OTTOMAN WOMEN
IN THE EYES OF WESTERN TRAVELERS

FİLİZ BARIN AKMAN

kopernik

FİLİZ BARIN AKMAN: She was born in 1982 in the Taşköprü region of the northern Anatolian province of Kastamonu. After completing her bachelor's degree at Middle East Technical University in Ankara, she went on to study at Illinois State University as a Fulbright scholar, completing her master's degree in English language and literature in 2006. Later, she completed her Ph.D. in 2014 at the same university with the dissertation "Orientalist Discourse(s): Western Representations of the Ottoman Society, Eastern Women and the Harem in Nineteenth Century Travel Writing, Fiction, and Art". She taught classes in the area of her expertise at Illinois State University between 2007 and 2013, and at the State University of New York at Geneseo in 2013 and 2014. Since 2015, she has been working as an academic at the Social Sciences University of Ankara Faculty of Foreign Languages Department of English Language and Literature. She has administered and presented papers at leading international conferences such as MLA, M/MLA and NeMLA. She has published articles in internationally prestigious, refereed journals and wrote a book in Turkish on the July 15, 2016 military coup attempt and the West's perception of the "other" and media studies titled, *Disinformation: How did the Western Media see Turkey's July 15 Coup Attempt? A Discourse Analysis: Orientalism, Neo-Imperialism and Islamophobia.* In addition to her main expertise on 19th century English Literature, she also studies post-Tanzimat era Ottoman history and literature, post-colonialism, women's studies, woman in the Ottoman Empire and Islam, media and cinema, and the "other" in the context of comparative literature and cultural studies. She is married and the mother of a very cute girl.

First published by Kopernik Publishing House
®Filiz Barın Akman 2018

All rights reserved to Dolmabahçe AŞ. Except for short excerpts for promoting purposes, it can not be distributed electronically or mechanically without the permission of the publisher. All the rights of this book are reserved to the author.

Editor in Chief: Abdülkadir Özkan
Advisor: Prof. Halil Berktay
Series Editor: Mehmet Erdoğan
Visual Director: Osman Özkan
Final Editing: Peter Klempner
Cover Design: Ali Kaya
Application:Tavoos

Kopernik Publishing House
Dolmabahçe AŞ
Altunizade Mah. Ord. Prof. Fahrettin Kerim Gökay Cad.34 Üsküdar
ISTANBUL
www.kopernikkitap.com

Certification no: 35175
ISBN: 978-975-2439-37-5
First Edition: January 2018

Publishing and Volume
Bilnet Matbaacılık ve Yayıncılık A.Ş.
Dudullu Organize San. Bölgesi 1.Cad. No:16 Ümraniye-ISTANBUL
Tel: 444 44 03 • Fax: (0216) 365 99 07 • www.bilnet.net.tr
Sertifika No: 31345

Kopernik Publishing House is a trade mark of Dolmabahçe AŞ
ISTANBUL • LONDON • NEW YORK

OTTOMAN WOMEN
IN THE EYES OF WESTERN TRAVELERS

FİLİZ BARIN AKMAN

kopernik

CONTENTS

FOREWORD   9

PART I
ORIGINS OF TRAVEL TO THE EAST   15
   The Crusades   17
   The Journey of Eastern Scientific Discoveries to the West   20
   Luxury Goods From the East to the West   22
   19th Century Travels to the Ottoman Empire   24
   The Eastern Origins of Coffee's Adventure   31

PART II
THE HAREM IN THE OTTOMAN EMPIRE AND THE DAILY LIVES OF WOMEN   41
   Women in Ottoman Society in the Eyes of Female Travelers   43
   Polygamy and the Concept of the Harem   49
   Free Women of the Ottoman Empire   55
   Place of Women in 19th Century British and Ottoman Societies   56
   Hamam As Women's Coffee Shop   69
   Status of Ottoman Women in the Eyes of Travelers   73
   Origins of Women's Rights in the Ottoman Empire   76
   Advancement of Women's Rights in Europe   77
   Women's Rights in the Ottoman Empire   85
   Divorce Law   88

CONCLUSION   103
REFERENCES   107

FOREWORD

Travel to the Middle East had become all the rage in many European countries in the 19th century. Travelers who usually visited cities under the dominion of the Ottoman Empire would almost without exception write about what they experienced and their impressions of the Eastern societies. Renowned cities and regions under Ottoman control, for example Cairo, Constantinople, Baghdad, Athens and Lebanon were always on the itinerary of these wondering travelers. Travel books on the Ottoman Empire written upon their return to their homelands often took readers to the unknown land of the Ottoman Empire and its mysterious people. These travelogues that tried to enlighten Western people on Middle Eastern societies, unfortunately, suffered from what Edward Said later identified through his concept of orientalism as obvious prejudice toward Middle Eastern societies, trying to portray the West as superior. Spreading exaggerated stories based on hearsay about the East is a centuries old tradition in the West dating back to the crusades of the Middle Ages and perpetuated through negative stereotypes.

In these books, the West defined itself through positive attributes like logic, science, civilization, humanity, intelligence, and ethics while identifying the East as the other, dismissing it as emotional, backward, archaic, barbaric, and lustful.

Said, while explaining orientalism, specifically delved into the historic roots of the process of the othering of the East, which reached a peak during 19th century British imperialism. He advises that all factors that affect society's perception, such as literature, art, media, and historiography, should always be interpreted in light of the dominant orientalist ideology.[1] In this context, what the West wrote about the East, its observations, literary works, history books, paintings, and travel books all carry the mark of the orientalist attitude the West holds for the East.

This study is based on travel books written about the Ottoman Empire in the 19th century when the British Empire had risen above the rest as the paramount imperial power of the world. The British Empire started to set up its globe-spanning network of colonies in the 19th century, while the fact that the most direct naval and land route to its crown jewel of India passed through the Ottoman Empire immensely increased British interest in the East. As the century forged ahead, so did Britain's coercive tactics to protect its special interests concerning Egypt, Cyprus, and the Arabian Peninsula. The fate of the Ottoman Empire suddenly became the most talked about topic among the British public, giving rise to the "Eastern Question".

In 1853, when the British Empire joined France to fight against tsarist Russia on the side of the Ottoman Empire in the Crimean War, was also when London suddenly became a very influential factor in the Sublime Porte.

The surge in interest in everything Ottoman came with

---

[1] Edward Said, *Orientalism*. New York: Vintage Books, 1994.

an increasing number of Westerners arriving in the Ottoman Empire, where they observed how people lived, the traditions and beliefs, and wrote about them once they returned home. However, these travelers-come-writers often distorted facts to portray the West as superior to anything out there in the Ottoman East. The West defined and gave form to an East as opposite in line with the later concept of orientalism.

Such attitudes are more apparent in men's writings that were fed by 19th century imperialist ideology. Conversely, women who traveled, such as Lady Mary Wortley Montagu, Julia Pardoe, Lady Emilia Bithynia Hornby, Annie Jane Harvey, and Sophia Lane-Poole, whose attitudes toward Ottoman women, their life at home, and Ottoman society at large was very different.[2] Such contrasting attitudes are one aspect Said ignored, as many academics have pointed out before.

Female writers showed a gentler, more understanding attitude toward the East. Books by female travelers are important concerning the daily lives of ordinary people, especially when it comes to women's status, women's rights, harems, and relations between men and women, all topics usually lost among the pages of Ottoman history.

As academics such as Billie Merman have noted, female travelers often used the status of women in Ottoman society to criticize the level of women's rights in 19th century Britain.

This is why this study includes a comparative analysis of Ottoman women's status in the eyes of Western travelers and divorce, marriage, and parental rights of women in the West as linked to the rise of feminism in 19th century Western societies.

This study aims to shine new light on women's place in

[2] For a more detailed discussion see Billie Melman, *Women's Orients: English Women and the Middle East, 1718-1918.* Ann Arbor: The University of Michigan Press, 1992.

Ottoman society, their daily lives, harems, marriage, divorce, and property ownership from the perspective of Western observers through detailed analysis of original travel books written at the time.

This study also includes samples of Western, orientalist painting traditions at appropriate points to support the narrative with special emphasis on how they influenced public attitudes.

This book contains two main headings. In the first section, a short historical summary of East-West relations is presented to provide a sound basis for the Western perception of Ottomans and Muslims. This is why in the first section I will explain the historical progress of East-West relations that began with the crusades. In this context, we will see how the East became a center of attraction for the West in subsequent centuries and the flow of advancements and developments from the East to the West. As an important example, coffee making and how it was transported from the Middle East to the West is described in detail with special references from travelers' notes.

While acknowledging the meanings and attributes carried by the concepts of the East and the West and the consequent criticism raised by thinkers of the problems that these pose, I try to use East and West, and Eastern and Western as they were used in the original 19th century texts.

The second section will take up Ottoman women in the eyes of Western travelers, which is the backbone of this study. Subheadings in this section include the status of women in the eyes of travelers, their rights, the harem, and their daily lives. Another subheading is the cooperative analysis of the perceived property and marital rights of women in Ottoman society and how women in Britain fared concerning the same rights. This is the first time Western travelers' observations are compiled in a single book. I believe it to be a colorful and valuable journey for those interested in the topic.

January, 2018 - ANKARA
Assistant Professor FİLİZ BARIN AKMAN

PART I
ORIGINS OF TRAVEL TO THE EAST

THE CRUSADES

Travels from the West to the East are not particular to the 19th century. Before tackling what 19th century travelers said or did, we need to go back several centuries to a time when Western Christians marched thousands of miles to make war on the East.

Having suffered a stinging defeat at the hands of the Seljuks at the Battle of Manzikert in 1071, the Byzantine Empire turned to the West and asked for help from Pope Urban II in 1094 or 1095. Almost all of Anatolia was under Seljuk control by then. Urban II, in his infamous sermon at the Council of Clermont in 1095, called on Christendom to mobilize against the East, and especially the Seljuks in Anatolia.

The sermon, which has several versions, calls Turks and Muslims as infidels, heathens, and enemies of Christianity, describing Muslims as members of a pagan religion. Turks and Muslims were accused of being barbaric murderers of Christians, who were called to stop infighting and unite to join the crusades to free their Christian brothers in the East. The pope, as the shadow of God on Earth, said those who joined and fought against Muslims would be absolved of all their sins.

An excerpt from the sermon demonstrates how it formed

the basis of the West's mistaken perception of Muslims and Turks. In the version of the sermon circulated by Fulcher of Chartre, pagans refer to Turks:

> All who die by the way, whether by land or by sea, or in battle against the pagans, shall have immediate remission of sins. This I grant them through the power of God which I am invested. O what a disgrace if such a despised and base race, which worships demands, should conquer a people which has the faith of omnipotent God and is made glorious with the name of Christ!
>
> With what reproaches will the Lord overwhelm us if you do not aid those who, with us, profess the Christian religion![1]

The version propagated by Robert the Monk almost 25 years later again described Turks as heathens, accusing them of fouling Constantinople and Jerusalem. It describes the Seljuk Empire of the late 11th to 12th century that controlled large parts of Anatolia, Iran, and Central Asia as the Persian Kingdom. It is full of so much disinformation that is accuses Turks of forcefully circumcising Christian men.

> From the confines of Jerusalem and the city of Constantinople a horrible tale has gone forth and very frequently has been brought to our ears, namely, that a race from the Kingdom of Persians, an accursed race, a race utterly alienated from God, a generation forsooth which has not directed its heart and has not entrusted its sprit to God, has invaded the lands of those Christians and has depopulated them by the sword, pillage and fire; it has led away a part of the captives into its own country, and a part it has destroyed by cruel tortures; it has either entirely destroyed the churches of God or appropriated them for the rites

---

[1] Bongars, *Gesta Dei per Francos*, 1, pp. 382 f., Oliver J. Thatcher and Edgar Holmes McNeal (ed.), *A Source Book for Medieval History*, New York: Scribners, 1905 an excerpt, pp. 513-517.

of its own religion. They destroy the altars, after having defiled them with their uncleanliness. They circumcise the Christians, and the blood of circumcision they either spread upon the altars or pour into the vases of the baptismal font.[2]

The rest of the sermon reads like a horror movie, accusing Turks of the utmost of barbarity, including raping Christian women.

When they wish to torture people by a base death, they perforate their navels, and dragging forth the extremity of the intestines, bind it to a stake; then with flogging they lead the victim around until the viscera having gushed forth the victim falls prostrate upon the ground. Others they compel to extend their necks and then, attacking them with naked swords, attempt to cut through the next with a single blow. What shall I say of the abominable rape of the women? To speak of it is worse than to be silent. The kingdom of Greeks is now dismembered by them and deprived of territory so vast in extent that it can not be traversed in a march of two months. On whom therefore is the labor of avenging these wrongs and of recovering this territory incumbent, if not upon you? You upon whom above other nations God has conferred remarkable glory in arms, great courage, bodily activity, and strength to humble the hairy scalp of those who resist you.[3]

The mass movement of soldiers from the West to recover Jerusalem from Muslims and to defend the Byzantine Empire from the Seljuks ushered the beginning of the Western public's introduction to the Muslim East.[4] Crusades continued for centuries, with Christian soldiers temporarily conquering Je-

---

[2] Dana C. Munro, "Urban and the Crusaders." Translations and Reprints from the Original Sources of European History, Vol 1:2, Philadelphia: University of Pennsylvania, 1895, pp. 5-8.
[3] ibid., pp. 5-8.
[4] Michael Paine, *The Crusades: History and Myths Revealed*, New York: Fall River Press, 2009, p. 32.

rusalem in 1099. Saladin, the sultan of Egypt and Syria, defeated a crusader army in the Battle of Hattin in 1187, and reconquered Jerusalem.

It was Ottoman Sultan Murad II's victory in the Battle of Varna in 1444 that finally extinguished the desire to go crusading on the part of Europeans.

The Journey of Eastern Scientific Discoveries to the West

If we momentarily leave aside the martial aspects of the crusades, it can easily be argued that the era started a large flow of scientific knowledge from the Middle East to the West and, as many historians can attest, ushered in the Renaissance.[5]

The crusades were the first time many poor members of the Christian public had the chance to leave impoverished Europe of the Dark Ages behind to see how people lived in the Middle East, which was experiencing a golden age. Many scientific ideas and devises long common in there found their way to the West thanks to soldiers and traders who knowingly or not became conduits to the process of Europe leaving the Middle Ages behind and entering the Renaissance. Military confrontation was slowly replaced by growing commercial and political ties. The advanced Muslim civilization started feeding the West's intellectual and commercial curiosity in many respects such as mathematics, art, silk, spices, and carpets.

One of the most important advancements that Europeans took from the East was the Arabic numeral system, which became one of the main foundations of the West's subsequent scientific advancement. Arabic numerals, which are very similar to the modern numerals used in the West, replaced Roman numer-

[5] ibid.

als and their very limited use in complex mathematical calculations. The introduction of the concept of zero, which originated in India, to the West via Arabs was, of course, a significant benefit, as Roman numerals lacked the number. Keeping in mind that all modern computing is founded on coding based on ones and zeros, one can start to imagine what the West, and consequently the entire world, owes to Muslim mathematicians.

The West also owes a great deal of gratitude to Western traders, especially from Venice and other Italian city-states, who maintained continuous commercial ties with their counterparts in the East. One of the most important was Italian trader Leonardo Pisano, also known as Fibonacci. He had the opportunity to travel the length and breadth of the Mediterranean Sea during late 12th century due to his father's occupation as a customs official in Algiers, and was taught by Arabic mathematicians about the Hindu-Arabic numeral system and understood how much easier it made calculations. Once he returned to Italy in 1202, he published the book *Lider Abaci*, or *The Book of Calculation*, explaining how Arabic numerals can be used.[6]

Algebra, one of the most important branches of mathematics, was also taken from the East. Algebra, or *al-jabr*, is part of the name of a book from 829 by ninth century Muslim Persian mathematician Muhammad ibn Musa al-Khwarizmi, based in Baghdad, *al-kitāb al-mukhtaṣar fī ḥisāb al-ğabr wa'l-muqābala* (*The Compendious Book on Calculation by Completion and Balancing*).[7] The word algorithm is derived from the Latinized version of his name al-Khwarizmi, Algoritmi.

Additionally, Abu Ali al-Ḥasan ibn al-Ḥasan ibn al-Hay-

---

[6] Jared Diamond, *1000 Events that Shaped the World*. Washington: National Geographic Society, 2007, p. 96.
[7] For detailed information, see John L. Esposito's *The Oxford History of Islam*, Oxford University Press.

tham, who died in Cairo in 1040, established the foundation on which the modern day lens and camera is based in his book *Kitāb al-Manāẓir* (*Book of Optics*). Astrologer Abu Abd Allah Muḥammad ibn Jabir ibn Sinan al-Raqqi al-Ḥarrani ash-Shabi al-Battani, or al-Battani, who was born in Harran in 858, calculated the solar year to near perfection, and was referred to by 15th century European astronomer Copernicus. Ibn Sina, or Avicenna as he is known in the West, wrote the medical book *al-Qānūn fī al-Ṭibb* (*The Canon of Medicine*), which was taught to doctors in the West for centuries to follow.

Luxury Goods From the East to the West

Many luxury goods also made their way to the West between the 11th and 15th centuries. It is no coincidence that many Renaissance paintings feature Ottoman and Persian carpets, as they had become a symbol of status for rich Europeans by then. Such carpets were not put on the floor but rather placed on tables to show their owners had traveled to the East.

German painter Holbein's 1533 painting *Ambassador*, which is in the collection of the National Gallery in London, displays all the objects they collected from the lands they visited over the years. The table in the middle is covered with a carpet of obvious Middle Eastern origins. The carpets in Holbein's paintings had become so famous during the Renaissance that the term "Holbein's carpets" came into being. Anatolian carpet motifs used in Renaissance era paintings were categorized in accordance with their geometric shapes under the heading of Holbein's carpets such as small or large motifs and lotto or rose motifs. For instance, those in *Ambassador* are in the category of large motifs. Holbein's portrait of

King Henry VIII of England also has an Anatolian carpet on the floor.[8]

Anatolian carpets are also often featured as decorative pieces in prominent Renaissance paintings of Jesus Christ and the Virgin Mary. Italian Renaissance painter Andrea del Verrocchio's *Madonna with Saint John the Baptist and Donatus* (circa 1475-1483) is among the most celebrated of such paintings.

Fabrics made from silk and other materials imported from the East also become popular among the rich and royalty. Fine muslin imported from Mosul in the Ottoman Empire entered the wardrobe of the famous 18th century Queen of France Mary Antoinette. She even posed for a painting in a dress made from this cloth. Her personal painter Élisabeth Louise Vigée Le Brun's 1783 painting *Marie Antoinette in a Muslin Dress* shows how Middle Eastern fabrics dominated some of the West's fashion trends as late as the 18th century. The same years also saw headscarves as a popular fashion accessory among European women. Headscarves worn by Ottoman women at home influenced French hat fashion so much that French women started to wear headscarves. Vigée Le Brun painted a portrait of herself wearing a headscarf and her child called *Self-Portrait in a Turban with Her Child*, as well as similar paintings of Marie Antoinette.

Lady Mary Wortley Montagu, an 18th century British travelogue writer, lived in Constantinople for a while and posed for quite a few paintings wearing Ottoman dresses, as "The Lure of the East: British Orientalist Painting" exhibit in 2009 at the Pera Museum displayed.

---

[8] Donald King and Sylvester David (eds.), *The Eastern Carpet in the Western World, from the 15th to the 17th century*. London: Arts Council of Great Britain, 1983.

19th Century Travels to the Ottoman Empire

If we return to the history of Westerners' travels to the East, we see a sudden climb in the number of adventurers braving the voyage. Poets, painters, and adventurers especially considered the journey eastward as a major source of inspiration. The image of the East created in *One Thousand and One Nights* is without doubt one reason behind the rise. It took centuries for the stories that told of the court of ninth century Caliph Harun al-Rashid to reach European shores. Antoine Galland published its first French translation in 1704. The first English translation was published exactly a decade later as *Arabian Nights*.

Many adventurers just wanted to see firsthand the storied cities, deserts, dresses, and characters in *One Thousand and One Nights* that fascinated them so much in their childhood. British Vanity Fair writer William Makepeace Thackeray refers to the *One Thousand and One Nights* many times in his 1846 book *A Journey from Cornhill to Grand Cairo*.

> If they love the odd and picturesque, if they loved the "Arabian Nights" in their youth, let them book themselves on board one of the Peninsular and Oriental vessels, and try one DIP into Constantinople or Smyrna. Walk into the bazaar, and the East is unveiled to you: how often and often have you tried to fancy this, lying out on a summer holiday at school! It is wonderful, too, how LIKE it is: you may imagine that you have been in the place before, you seem to know it so well! [9]

Many poets and adventurers posed for paintings wearing Anatolian or Arabic clothing they purchased during their Ottoman travels. British poet Lord Byron (1788-1824) posed in an Albanian outfit for a portrait in 1813 by Thomas Philipps,

---

[9] William Makepeace Thackeray, *Notes of a Journey From Cornhill to Grand Cairo*. New York: Wiley & Putnam, 1846, p. 48.

Lord Byron in Albanian Dress, which is among the most famous. The poet later joined the Greeks in their rebellion against the Ottoman Empire and died after contracting a fever during battle at age 36, transforming into another symbol of inspiration for many who followed him. The name of his famous poem *Giour* is derived from the Ottoman word *gâvur*, which means infidel.

Another example of Westerners posing in Ottoman garb is Sir Joshua Reynolds' *Mrs Baldwin in Eastern Dress*. Jane Baldwin was born in 1763 to a British family living in Smyrna, present-day Izmir. She later married a rich merchant before moving to Britain, where she was very conspicuous at balls for wearing Ottoman dresses.

Nineteenth century British writer and adventurer Henry Pickersgill, who traveled throughout the Ottoman Empire, published *Travels in Palestine* in 1821, and two years later, *Travels Among the Arab Tribes*, before commissioning the painting in 1825 for which he and his wife posed with Ottoman clothing.

Major advancements in transportation in the 19th century, including railroads and steamships, not only helped to increase the number of travelers to the East, but also allowed many more women to undertake the previously risky voyage.

The sudden rise in the number of women writing books about their travels brought a breath of fresh air on the way the East was portrayed in the West. At a time when men could perceive what they saw only through the patronizing lens of imperialism, the change of focus women provided deserves a detailed comparative analysis.

Edward Freeman, in his book, *Turks in Europe*, published in 1877, uses multiple abusive terms when describing "the

Turks." It is interesting to note that the language is surprisingly similar to the one used by the Roman Catholic Church almost a millennium before to find recruits for the crusades.

> What have the Turks done In Europe?
>
> This question might be answered in a few words. They have destroyed and they have oppressed. They have checked all progress in a large part of Europe. They have made promises and have broken them. They have shown themselves cruel, lustful, and faithless, even beyond other barbarian conquerors. This is all true in a general way ; but it will be well to go a little more into detail, and to give a short sketch of the history of the Ottoman power, of its rise, and its decline.[10]

Christian missionary Archibald McLean, who visited the Ottoman Empire in the 19th century for the Foreign Christian Missionary Society, used hateful language in his travelogue to describe his feelings toward the Turks, calling for their immediate cleansing from Europe. He begins by sharing his sadness over the Hagia Sofia having been converted into a mosque, expressing his anticipation for the day when it is converted back into a church.

> Mohammed II took Constantinople in 1453. Since that time it has been the seat of Turkish Government, religious and secular. Saint Sophia has been changed into a mosque. This great church was built by Justinian. Columns were taken from the temple of Diana in Ephesus, from Aurelian's temple of the Sun, and from Egypt. When the building was completed, the Emperor said: "Glory to God, who hath thought me worthy to accomplish so great a work ! I have vanquished thee, O Solomon!" A good judge pronounces it the fairest and noblest church in the world. The Greeks said

---

[10] Edward Freeman, *Turks in Europe*. New York Harper and Brothers Publishers, 1877, p. 31.

to the Russian envoys: "What ! do you not know that the angels come down from heaven to mingle in our services?" This noble structure was defaced and defiled. Minarets were erected and other additions made to adapt it to Mohammedan worship. But Saint Sophia was a church, and, please God, it shall be a church again. Mosques have been built in all parts of the city. They are by far the most conspicuous objects in the whole landscape. There can be no doubt as to the dominant faith in Constantinople. The city of Constantine and Theodosius and Justinian and Chrysostom is the most thoroughly Mohammedan city in Europe or Asia, with the exception of Mecca. The Sultan is not only an absolute monarch, but Khaliff as well. The whole Mohammedan world, with the single exception of Persia, look to him as their spiritual guide. Not only so, but the Greek and Armenian Patriarchs and the chief Rabbi of the Jews live there. While I was in Constantinople, I could not but deplore that the feuds of Christian people enabled the Turk to enter Europe. For the Turk in Europe is as much out of place as a pig in a parlor. The Turks were converted to Islam while they were savages. Islam arrests development; consequently the Turks are where they were a thousand years ago. They have a thin veneer of civilization, and by courtesy they are called civilized, but they are not. In policy and in practice the Turk is a savage. He is not a builder : he is a destroyer. Asia Minor has been desolated. Ephesus is a ruin. Nicea is a village. Hundreds of towns and cities have disappeared; mines have been deserted. People do not raise more than enough to support life. The nerve of endeavor has been cut. All incentives to enterprise and economy have been done away. The countries under Turkish control are capable of supporting ten times their present population.[11]

Famous writer William Makepeace Thackeray, in his

---

[11] Archibald McLean, *A Circuit of the Globe*. St. Louis: Christian Publishing Company, 1897, pp. 344-345.

book about his 1844 travels to Athens, Smyrna, Constantinople and Cairo, observes the East through the typical orientalist point of view of the time, constantly trying to emphasize the West's superiority over the East. He describes the British as lions and the Ottoman sultan and governor of Jaffa as rascals.

> What I would urge, humbly, however, is this—Do not let us be led away by German writers and aesthetics, Semilassoisms, Hahnhahnisms, and the like. The life of the East is a life of brutes. The much maligned Orient, I am confident, has not been maligned near enough; for the good reason that none of us can tell the amount of horrible sensuality practised there.[12]

It was Lady Mary Wortley Montagu (1675-1739), having arrived in Constantinople in the early 18th century with her husband, the newly appointed British ambassador, who began the women travelogue tradition about the East. Her famous *The Turkish Embassy Letters* is an observational masterpiece of her two years in Constantinople and displays her sympathetic attitude that lacks any orientalist underpinnings toward Muslim traditions and daily life. Her letters, which form the book, include long descriptions of what she observed of the daily lives of ordinary people in Constantinople as well as medical developments she witnessed.

Having lost her brother to smallpox, Lady Montagu saw it as her patriotic duty to share among her compatriots the knowledge of vaccinations that Ottoman doctors employed against the disease. She personally oversaw the vaccination of her children while in Constantinople. At first, her efforts received a significant backlash. As the foreword for the 1869

---

[12] William Makepeace Thackeray, *Notes of a Journey From Cornhill to Grand Cairo.* New York: Wiley & Putnam, 1846, p. 265

edition of her book explains, in the early 18th century, every one in seven people died from smallpox in Britain, and survivors lived their lives marked with deep scars. Still, she encountered serious opposition.

Academics objected and religious figures described what she was doing as opposing God's will and accused her of being a heretic. Ordinary people were told to shout vulgarities to such a woman who would risk the lives of her children. The reaction was so severe that Montagu, despite her evident courage for humanity's progress, might have dropped the whole matter if she had foreseen how she would be treated.[13]

Still, the smallpox vaccination Lady Montagu brought to Britain in the 1720s entered Western medical literature despite all opposition. In 1821, soon after Lady Montagu publicized the smallpox vaccine she learned of while in Constantinople, a smallpox outbreak griped London. The royal family, having heard of Lady Montagu's vaccine, considered it for their protection. As their doctors advised against the vaccine, the royal family decided to use the vaccine initially on people on death row. After the inmates recovered in a few weeks, the royal family decided to get vaccinated, becoming the foremost supporters of the procedure for the British public.[14] According to records, a dramatic decrease was seen soon afterward in deadly smallpox cases in the country.

Lady Montagu describes the smallpox vaccine in her letters:

> I am going to tell you a thing that I am sure will make you wish yourself here. The small-pox, so fatal, and so general amongst us, is here entirely harmless by the invention of ingrafting,

---

[13] Lady Montagu, *Letters of Lady Mary Wortley Montagu*. Sarah Josepha Hale (ed.), Boston: Roberts Brothers, 1869, Preface xiv.
[14] ibid.

which is the term they give it. There is a set of old women who make it their business to perform the operation every autumn, in the month of September, when the great heat is abated. People send to one another to know if any of their family has a mind to have the small-pox: they make parties for this purpose, and when they are met (commonly fifteen or sixteen together), the old woman comes with a nut-shell full of the matter of the best sort of small- pox, and asks what veins you please to have opened. She immediately rips open that you offer to her with a large needle (which gives you no more pain than a common scratch), and puts into the vein as much venom as can lie upon the head of her needle, and after binds up the little wound with a hollow bit of shell; and in this manner opens four or five veins. The Grecians have commonly the superstition of opening one in the middle of the forehead, in each arm, and on the breast, to mark the sign of the cross; but this has a very ill effect, all these wounds leaving little scars, and is not done by those that are not superstitious, who choose to have them in the legs, or that part of the arm that is concealed. The children or young patients play together all the rest of the day, and are in perfect health to the eighth. Then the fever begins to seize them, and they keep their beds two days, very seldom three. They have very rarely above twenty or thirty in their faces, which never mark ; and in eight days' time they are as well as before their illness. Where they are wounded, there remain running sores during the distemper, which I don't doubt is a great relief to it. Every year thousands undergo this operation; and the French embassador says pleasantly, that they take the small-pox here by way of diversion, as they take the waters in other countries. There is no example of any one that has died in it ; and you may believe I am very well satisfied of the safety of the experiment, since I intend to try it on my dear little son. I am patriot enough to take pains to bring this useful invention into fashion in England; and I should not fail to write to some of our doctors very particularly about it, if I knew any one of them that I thought had virtue enough to destroy such a considerable branch of their revenue for the good of mankind.[15]

In her letters, Lady Montagu endeavored to correct the distorted image of the Turk and the East in the minds of Europeans. Her observations compelled many to revisit their impression of Turks as barbarians, which had remained unchanged since the conquest of Constantinople and much of southeastern Europe. For example, she criticized the barbarian image by describing the kindness with which Turks treated their slaves working in their households.

> I know you'll expect I should say something particular of that of the slaves; and you will imagine me half a Turk when I don't speak of it with the same horror other Christians have done before me. But I cannot forbear applauding the humanity of the Turks to these creatures; they are never ill- used, and their slavery is, in my opinion, no worse than servitude all over the world.[16]

The Eastern Origins of Coffee's Adventure

Among all the things the West acquired from the East, coffee most assuredly has a special place. Coffee's journey gives us a glimpse into interaction between civilizations. Almost every traveler whose books track women's place in the Ottoman Empire mention this concoction, which provides a clue of the cultural interactions between all, from senior administrators to ordinary folk. On their return trips, Western travelers brought with them much clothing,

---

[15] Lady Montagu, *Letters of Lady Mary Wortley Montagu*, Sarah Josepha Hale (ed.), Boston: Roberts Brothers, 1869, p. 358-359.
[16] ibid.

foodstuffs, spices, and other articles of interest used in the daily lives of the people of the Ottoman Empire.

Coffee is probably the most far-reaching of all the items taken from the East to the West. Coffee, which originated in Ethiopia, was first brought to Constantinople in early 16th century. The Turkish proverb, the best coffee comes from Yemen, is an indication of how it came to the capital of Ottoman Empire. Coffee, which comes from an Arabic word, was popularized in the metropolitan centers of the empire such Damascus, Mecca, and Constantinople. The first real coffee shops opened in Damascus in 1530, before spreading to Cairo, and in 1554 to Constantinople. By the end of the century, there were around 600 coffee shops.[17]

Edward Lane, a professor of Arabic who lived in Ottoman Cairo in early 19th century, describes the history of coffee as follows:

> The cup of coffee, which, when it can be afforded, generally accompanies the pipe, is commonly regarded as an almost equal luxury, and doubtless conduced with tobacco to render the use of wine less common among the Arabs: its name, "kahweh," an old Arabic term for wine, strengthens this supposition. It is said that the discovery of the refreshing beverage afforded by the berry of the coffee-plant was made in the latter part of the seventh century of the Flight (or, of the thirteenth of the Christian era), by a certain devotee named the sheykh 'Omar, who, driven by persecution to a mountain of El-Yemen, with a few of his disciples, was induced, by the want of provisions, to make an experiment of the decoction of coffee-berries, as an article of food ; the coffee-plant being there a spontaneous production.

[17] Francis B.C. Thurnber, *Coffee from Plantation to Cup: A Brief History of Coffee Production and Consumption* (9th ed.). New York: American Grocer Publishing Association, 1884.

It was not, however, till about two centuries after this period that the use of coffee began to become common in El-Yemen. It was imported into Egypt between the years 900 and 910 of the Flight (towards the end of the fifteenth or the beginning of the sixteenth century of our era, or about a century before the introduction of tobacco into the East), and was then drunk in the great mosque El-Azhar, by the fakeers of El-Yemen and Mekkeh and El-Medeeneh, who found it very refreshing to them while engaged in their exercises of reciting prayers, and the praises of God, and freely indulged themselves with it. About half a century after, it was introduced into Constantinople. In Arabia, in Egypt, and in Constantinople, it was often the subject of sharp disputes among the pious and learned ; many doctors asserting that it possessed intoxicating qualities, and was, therefore, an unlawful beverage to Muslims ; while others contended that, among many other virtues, it had that of repelling sleep, which rendered it a powerful help to the pious in their nocturnal devotions : according to the fancy of the ruling power, its sale was therefore often prohibited and again legalized.

It is now, and has been for many years, acknowledged as lawful by almost all the Muslims, and is immoderately used even by the Wahhabees, who are the most rigid in their condemnation of tobacco, and in their adherence to the precepts of the Kuran, and the Traditions of the Prophet. Formerly, it was generally prepared from the berries and husks together ; and it is still so prepared, or from the husks alone, by many persons in Arabia. In other countries of the East, it is prepared from the berries alone, freshly roasted and pounded.

The coffee-shops are most frequented in the afternoon and evening; but by few except persons of the lower orders, and tradesmen. The exterior mastabah is generally preferred. Each person brings with him his own tobacco and pipe. Coffee is served by the "kahwegee" (or attendant of the shop), at the price of five faddahs a cup, or ten for a little "bekreg" (or pot) of three or four cups. The kahwegee also keeps two or three nargeelehs or sheeshehs, and gdzehs, which latter are used for smoking both the tumbak (or Persian tobacco) and the hasheesh (or hemp) ; for hasheesh is sold at some coffee-shops.[18]

Thanks to Italian and Venetian traders, coffee, and consequently coffee shops, spread first to Italy in the 16th century, with the first coffee shop opening in 1645. In subsequent decades, Ottoman influence led to coffee consumption spreading across much of the continent, where it was promoted as the East Brew.

Pope Clement VIII even went so far as to ban coffee as the "Muslim drink", bringing to mind the way Europeans dismissed the Ottoman smallpox vaccine as a "Muslim treatment" when Lady Montagu first introduced it around a century later.

The first English word for coffee was *chaoua* in 1598. The first coffee shop in Britain was opened in Corhnhill, London in 1652 by a Greek named Pasqua Rossie. Rumors say that Rossie, who used to work for a British trader, carried coffee during one travel from Smyrna to Britain. Friends and guests soon flood the trader's home, looking for a sip of the new drink. However, he soon tired of all the commotion and decided to open a shop where he would not be bothered by the comings and goings of customers.[19]

By the late 17th century, there was a sudden increase in the number of coffee shops in Britain. Travelers, however, constantly noted the huge difference in quality between Turkish

---

[18] Edward William Lane, *The Manners and Customs of the Modern Egyptians* (23. ed.). London: J. M. Dent and Co., 1908 (1. ed. 1836), pp. 339-340.
[19] Francis B.C. Thurber, *Coffee from Plantation to Cup: A Brief History of Coffee Production and Consumption* (9. ed.). New York: American Grocer Publishing Association, 1884, p. 54.

and local brews. Austrian soldiers, after seizing the bags of coffee Ottoman soldiers brought with them to the siege of Vienna, popularized it across the city. The Ottoman soldiers could not take the city, but the coffee beans they brought certainly did.

Thanks to travelers and traders, coffee reached became known in France in 1658. According to Francis Thurber's book on the history of coffee, French traveler Jean de Thévenot, on his return from the East, treated his guests to a delicious round of coffee after dinner.[20]

Coffee's renown spread even further across France after Ottoman Sultan Mehmed IV sent a delegation in 1669, headed by Suleiman Pasha to French King Louis XIV. Among the presents given to the French king were an embroidered pitcher, rosewater, and Turkish delight. Afterward, vendors dressed in Ottoman clothing started to sell coffee on the streets.[21] Thurber's book, the ninth edition of which was published in 1884, explains how coffee suddenly became popular toward the end of the 17th century France.

> This circumstance occurred on the arrival, in 1669, of an embassy from the Grand Seigneur Mahomet IV to Louis XIV Soliman Aga, chief of the mission, having passed six months in the capital, and during his stay having acquired the friendship of the Parisians by some traits of wit and gallantry, several persons of distinction, chiefly women, had the curiosity to visit him at his house. The manner in which he received them not only inspired a wish to renew the visit, but induced others to follow the example. He caused coffee to be served to his guests, according to the custom of his country; for since fashion had introduced the custom of serving this beverage among the Turks, civility de-

---
[20] ibid.
[21] ibid.

manded that it should be offered to visitors, as well as that these should not decline partaking of it. [22]

Thurber also notes the importance of grace in the presentation of coffee while commenting on the fearsome strength of the Ottoman Empire of the time.

> If a Frenchman, in a similar case, to please the ladies, had presented to them this black and bitter liquor, he would have been rendered forever ridiculous. But the beverage was served by a Turk—a gallant Turk—and this was sufficient to give it inestimable value. Besides, before the palate could judge, the eyes were seduced by the display of elegance and neatness which accompanied it; by those brilliant porcelain cups into which it was poured; by napkins with gold fringes, on which it was served to the ladies. Add to this the furniture, the dresses, and the foreign customs, the strangeness of addressing the host through the interpreter, being seated on the ground, on tiles, etc., and you will allow that there was more than enough to turn the heads of his visitors. Leaving the hotel of the ambassador with an enthusiasm easily imagined, they hastened to their acquaintances, to speak of the coffee of which they had partaken; and Heaven only knows to what a degree they were excited. "Marseilles lays claim to the first coffee-house in France, 1671. In the following year, an Armenian, named Pascal, opened a shop at the Fair of Saint-Germain, near Paris, in which he dispensed the exotic beverage to the sightseers.[23]

Still, despite the fact that coffee was first introduced to France in the late 17th century, French Colonel E. Napier's astonished reaction to the beverage, as if he were seeing it for the first time while traveling in the Ottoman Empire in the 1840s, shows that its spread was still limited.

Colonel Napier entered a coffee shop while he was waiting

---

[22] ibid.
[23] ibid., pp. 55-56

for the ship that would take him to Constantinople from Smyrna. This is how he describes the coffee and the shop owner.

> I took refuge in a " cafanet," and, with a narghili and coffee, beguiled away the time; in this I was assisted by the musical propensity of mine host, a finelooking old Moslem, who, in the ancient garb of the faithful—the ample turban and flowing robes—was amusing his audience with the monotonous sounds of a sort of guitar, which is known here by the name of a " sas." The " cafanet " is as much, or perhaps more, resorted to by the idlers in the Levant, than the " cabaret " in France, or the " cafe " in Spain. Here, for a few paras, stretched at his ease, or seated cross-legged on one of the raised platforms which surround the apartment, the Turk can enjoy those greatest luxuries of his existence—the essence of the " berry, "* and the aroma of his chibouk; whilst for hours he will sit, the most contented of human beings, sipping the one, and inhaling the fumes of the other. * Coffee, that " brew " for which the Turks are so celebrated, is made by them in the following simple manner:—A small vessel, containing about a wine-glass of water, is placed on the fire, and when boiling, a teaspoonful of ground coffee is put into it, stirred up, and it is suffered to boil and " bubble " a few seconds longer, when it is poured (grounds and all) into a cup about the size of an egg-shell, encased in gold or silver filigree work, to protect the finger from the heat; and the liquid, in its scalding, black, thick, and troubled state, is imbibed with the greatest relish. Like smoking, it must be quite an acquired taste, and the quaint remarks on the subject of old Spon and Wheeler are very amusing.[24]

Nineteenth century travelers continued to comment on Turkish coffee in their writings, demonstrating that the drink

---

[24] E. Colonel Napier, *Excursions Along the Shores of the Mediterranean, vol. II.* London: Henry Colburn Publisher, 1842, p. 337.

was still less than conspicuous in Europe at the time. British traveler Julia Pardoe wrote about her pleasant experience of drinking a delicious cup of Turkish coffee at the home in which she was a guest before visiting Sultanahmet Mosque with her father and Ottoman servants, lamenting the failure of European coffee connoisseurs to replicate the taste.[25]

Halil Hadid, one of whose ancestors worked as an imam at the Haci Bektaşi Veli Mosque and Madrasah in Ankara during the reign of Sultan Murad II (1404-1451), lived in Britain for a while in the 19th century. He also compared the local brew unfavorably to the one back home, explaining that coffee was one of the things he missed the most.[26]

Sophia Poole, who lived in Cairo, wrote about the presentation of coffee in Egyptian Governor Mehmed Ali Pasha's harem in 1843, which she experienced during a visit. She explains in detail how they were welcomed into the room of pasha's wife in the harem, where they sat on sofas before they were presented with cups of coffee and pieces of Turkish delight on silver trays. As beautiful scents enveloped the guests, rosewater was offered for those in need of refreshment.[27]

During the Crimean War in 1853, Lady Emilia Bithynia Hornby, the wife of a British official sent to the Ottoman capital as head of the commission overseeing the structuring of state debt, wrote about the coffee presentation ceremony she experienced with a friend as a guest in Rıza Pasha's harem.

> Coffee ceremony: and on the principal wife clapping her hands, some richly-dressed slaves brought in trays of conserves, and

---

[25] Julia Pardoe, *The City of the Sultan and Domestic Manners of the Turks with a Steam Voyage up to Danube* (4th ed.). London: G. Routledge & Co.. 1854, p. 165.

[26] Halil Hamid, *The Diary of a Turk*. London: Adam and Charles Black. 1903, p. 244.

[27] Sophia Poole, *The Englishwoman in Egypt: Letters From Cairo*. Azza Kararah (ed.) Egypt: The American University in Cairo Press, 2003, p. 131.

water in crystal cups. On the first tray is a glass vase of the conserve, with a beautiful silver basket on either side of it, one of which is filled with spoons of the same metal. You take a spoonful of sweetmeat, and then place the spoon which you have used, in the empty basket on the other side. Then another slave presents you with a richly-cut cup of water. After that the coffee-bearers enter. One of them holds a tray of semicircular form, from which hangs a magnificently embroidered and fringed cloth of gold. Other slaves then take the coffee and present it to each guest. The outer cup is exactly like an egg-cup; inside this, is one of the finest china, which contains the beverage. We admired their outer cups immensely; they were of richly chased gold, encircled with diamonds about an inch apart and the size of a large pea.[28]

Coffee's journey around the world ended in the New World, with U.S. companies Starbucks and Gloria Jeans retracing the journey to where coffee drinking originated.

---

[28] Emilia Bithynia Hornby, *In and Around Stamboul*. Philedelphia: James Challen & Son, 1918 (1. ed. 1858), p. 252.

PART II
THE HAREM IN THE OTTOMAN EMPIRE AND THE DAILY LIVES OF WOMEN

WOMEN IN OTTOMAN SOCIETY IN THE EYES OF FEMALE TRAVELERS

Many women who traveled to the Ottoman Empire in the 19th century followed in the earlier footsteps of Lady Montagu, and some of the most prominent topics they covered were Ottoman women and harems, Ottoman women's place in the family and society, and relations between men and women. Contrary to their male counterparts, female travel writers were able to easily gain access to harems, allowing them a much sounder perspective on internal family dynamics in the Ottoman Empire.

Edward Lane (1801-1876), a professor of Arabic who compiled an Arabic-English dictionary and was one of the foremost translators of *Arabian Nights*, lived in Cairo, which was an Ottoman province at the time. While he continued his studies in Cairo from 1825 on, he invited his sister Sophia Lane-Poole to live with him to gain a perspective on life in the harem through her. Lane-Poole also contributed to the growing literature by publishing her account in her 1838 book, *Englishwomen in Egypt*. Professor Lane's studies produced *Manners and Customs of the Modern Egyptians in 1836, published by the Society for the Diffusion of Useful Knowledge.

Another important female traveler was Julia Pardoe (1806-1862), who lived in Constantinople for two years. She first accompanied her father to the city in 1836, and had the opportunity to visit many parts, including several harems. Her observations were published in two books, *The City of the Sultan: Domestic Manners of the Turks* and *The Beauties of the Bosphorus*.

About 17 years after Pardoe, Lady Emilia Bithynia Hornby, arrived in Constantinople with her British diplomat husband. Her book, *In and Around Stanboul*, presents her observations of the city and Ottoman society at large during the Crimean War. Annie Jane Harvey's 1871 book, *Turkish Harems and Circassian Homes*, which she wrote after her stay in Constantinople, is another travelogue published around the same time.

What differentiates female travel writers from their male counterparts is their ability to gain access to harem life, allowing them to present their close observations of family and Ottoman women, which is definitely lacking in books by men. In addition to detailed descriptions of women's dress and celebratory garments, most of what these women wrote about focused on how Ottoman women lived and life in the previously baffling harem.

These women who traveled to the Ottoman Empire in the 18th and 19th centuries, to the best of their abilities, answered the questions such as what was the status of women in Ottoman society and family life and were women imprisoned in harems – topics that continue to spark furious debates in modern Turkey. They usually try to compare women's life in the Ottoman Empire to the life many of their compatriots led back home. For example, the status of women in Ottoman society and the value given them surprised most female travelers, as did the surprising discovery that Ottoman women enjoyed many freedoms denied women in the West. Contrary to belief, they argued that Ottoman women were not slaves imprisoned in harems, but rather had definite rights vis-a-vis their husbands.[1]

While most books are dotted with remarks that demonstrate orientalist arrogance and the prevailing British imperial attitude of superiority, they also contain many passages that shine a light on many previously obscure historical facts.

Additionally, female writers provide a healthier alternative then the books published by their male counterparts, which are filled with fantasies rather than facts about life in harems and Ottoman women.

Many Western painters depicted Ottoman women in harems and baths, in erotic poses, or making suggestive gestures, the most famous of which are members of the French orientalist school Eugene Delacroix (1798-1863) and Jean-Léon Gerome (1824-1904). These artists' paintings perfectly summarize the prejudices about the East dominant in their society and follow the usual orientalist inclinations. The underlying message is the East has a mysterious culture in the grip of sensuality, but also governed by violence and barbarity.[2]

As mentioned before, Lady Montagu, who lived in Constantinople from 1718 to 1720, shared her impressions with

---

[1] For more detailed information on the issue, see Fariba Zarinebaf-Shahr's *Women, Law and Imperial Justice*, p. 82. She cites examples by using the Complaints Documents stored by the Prime Ministry to explain the influence of Ottoman women in the 17th, 18th, and 19th centuries.

[2] For a detailed criticism of orientalist painting see Lynne Thornton, *Women as Portrayed in Orientalist Painting*, Paris: ACR PocheCouleur, 1994.

her friends and family back home, including writer Alexander Pope, and opened the space for female traveler writers with her published letters. Her observations and experiences belie even modern Turkish society's misconceptions about the era. *The Turkish Embassy Letters* include observations about the status of Ottoman women and life in the harem that are surprising, to say the least. Contrary to previous misconceptions, Ottoman women were hardly imprisoned slaves, Lady Montagu says, constantly arguing that they enjoyed many rights and freedoms that Western women lacked. The most important topics she mentions are the right to purchase and manage property and the right to divorce given to women as per Islamic law. The image of Eastern women living in harems under the constant oppression of men could not be further from the truth:

> 'Tis also very pleasant to observe how tenderly he [the traveller, Aaron Hill], and all his brethren voyage-writers lament the miserable confinement of the Turkish ladies, who are perhaps freer than any ladies in the universe, and are the only women in the world that lead a life of uninterrupted pleasure exempt from cares; their whole time being spent in visiting, bathing, or the agreeable amusement of spending money, and inventing new fashions. A husband would be thought mad that exacted any degree of economy from his wife, whose expenses are no way limited but by her own fancy. 'Tis his business to get money, and hers to spend it: and this noble prerogative extends itself to the very meanest of the sex.[3]

As number of travelers to the Ottoman Empire increased dramatically in the 19th century, John Murray published a travel guide, *For Travellers in Constantinople and Turkey in Asia*, whose fourth edition in 1878 mentions life in the harem

---

[3] Lady Montagu, p. 168.

and explains how misconstrued the impression is that women are imprisoned in them.

> It is an error to suppose that Turkish women are imprisoned in their houses like birds in a cage. On the contrary, they have in some respects more liberty than European women. They roam about at will through the Bazaars, and they drive through the streets, disguised in a costume which renders recognition impossible. They are veiled, and cover their whole persons with the ferefgee, so that it is impossible to distinguish one female from another. The wives of Turks of rank are always accompanied by a eunuch; others who cannot afford that luxury go about alone.[4]

Julia Pardone, who lived in Constantinople in 1836 and wrote the book *City of the Sultan: Domestic Manners of the Turks*, says that titles such as *sultan* or *effendi* are not exclusively used for men, but also commonly used for women, and argues that such behavior denotes greater gender equality in the Ottoman Empire. The rights and freedoms enjoyed by Ottoman women, she says, are not known in the West, and as such, allows mistaken impressions of the facts to govern the attitude of the majority in the West.

> If, we are all prone to believe, freedom be happiness, then are the Turkish women the happiest, for they are certainly the freest individuals in the Empire. It is the fashion in Europe to pity the women of the East; but it is ignorance of their real position alone which can engender so misplaced an exhibition of sentiment. I have already stated that they are permitted to expostulate, to urge, even to insist on any point they may feel an interest: nor does an Osmanli husband ever resent the expressions of

---

[4] John Murray, *Handbook for Travellers in Constantinople and Turkey in Asia* (4. ed.). London: John Murray Firm, 1878, p. 96.

his wife; it is on the contrary, part and parcel of his philosophy to bear the storm of words unmoved; and the most emphatic and passionate oration of the inmates of his harem seldom produces more than the trite "Bakalum - we shall see."[5]

Just like Pardoe, Sophia Lane-Poole, who lived in Ottoman Cairo between 1842 and 1844, also argues that the rights and freedoms enjoyed by women in the East are greater than those enjoyed by their counterparts in the West.

I have been exceedingly amused lately, by reading in The Sketches of Persia, the account given by some natives of that country (including persons occupying high offices under government, therefore the noble of the land) of the liberty and power of their women; and I am disposed to think with them, that women, in many respects, have the ascendency among the higher orders throughout the East. We imagine in England that the husband in these regions is really lord and master, and he is in some cases; but you will scarcely believe that the master of the house may be excluded for many days from his own hareem, by his wife or wives causing a pair of slippers to be placed outside the door, which signifies that there are visitors within.[6]

Lane-Poole, with her firsthand observations in Cairo, disproves the assumption, spread mostly by men, that harems are akin to prisons for women.

The middle classes are at liberty to pay visits, and go to the bath, when they please; but their fathers and husbands object to their shopping; therefore female brokers are in the frequent habit of attending the hareems. The higher orders are more closely guarded, yet as this very circumstance is a mark of distinction, the women congratulate each other on this subject; and it is not

---

[5] Pardoe, p. 96.
[6] Sophia Lane-Poole, p. 119.

uncommon for a husband to give his wife a pet name, expressive of her hidden charms such as "the concealed jewel". [7]

Lane-Poole's brother, famous orientalist Edward Lane, in his book *Manners and Customs of the Modern Egyptians*, also argues that women in harems are not imprisoned, mentioning working women in Egypt who come predominantly from the lower classes.

> Some women, in the towns, keep shops, and sell bread, vegetables, etc.; and thus contribute as much as their husbands, or even more than the latter, to the support of their families.[8]

Polygamy and the Concept of the Harem

One of the aspects of the East most criticized in the West is the presence of polygamy. Some Western observers, including Florence Nightingale (1820-1910) who worked as a nurse in Constantinople during the Crimean War, argued that polygamy was too widespread in Eastern societies and this constituted a grave danger to the wellbeing of women. Those who had access to harems, however, came to the conclusion that polygamy was not as prevalent as first thought. British Colonel Charles White, who stayed in Constantinople for three years, in his book *Three Years in Constantinople*, said:

> The philosopher will find, in this custom of indulgence, and its antecedents, causes more potent than polygamy or plague for the slow progress of population, when compared with other countries. It is admitted by medical men and others, who have strictly investigated the extent of polygamy in the capital, where the practice forms the exception and not the rule that, were it not for

---

[7] ibid., p. 116
[8] Edward Lane, p. 199.

the foregoing causes, the population would increase rapidly, in spite of the efforts made to counteract nature, and of other causes that militate against the propagation of the species, of which plague is not the least powerful.* The mortality among children in the richest families and most favoured positions doubles that of any other country. On seeking into the causes of death, they are, with few exceptions, to be discovered in inflammatory complaints, arising from the circumstances above mentioned.[9]

Halil Halid's book, *A Diary of a Turk*, likewise, in the section that mentions polygamy in the East, explains all the responsibilities men have for their wives. He also lists all the reasons behind why polygamy is not that common in the Ottoman Empire.

Religion, law, and custom impose upon men many duties to be discharged towards their wives. An honest man must discharge these duties, and indeed it is very difficult to find many men who are able to fulfill their obligations as husbands towards more than one wife. It has been proved that in many parts of the Ottoman empire the number of women does not exceed that of men, a fact which alone is enough to show the absurdity of the notion prevailing in England about the plurality of wives in that country.[10]

Lady Montagu also dismisses the widespread prevalence of polygamy in the Ottoman Empire of early 18^{t}h century, adding that the man of the household did not have sexual relations with every woman living in the harem. She says that while husbands have the right to marry four women, there are very few women of means who would allow their husbands to do so.[11]

Mrs. Harvey, in her 1871 book, *Turkish Harems and Circas-*

---

[9] Charles White, *Three Years in Constantinople, Volume 3.* 1845, p. 7.
[10] Halil Halid, pp. 46-49.
[11] Montagu, p. 80.

sian Homes, corroborates what Pardoe [12] and Halid said about the rarity of polygamy in Ottoman society. She says, "In this harem, as is now generally the case in the best Turkish families, there is but one wife."[13]

Local and foreign studies on Ottoman society also found public documents that show that polygamy was indeed very rare. According to census figures from 1848 Cairo, only 2.7 percent of men were polygamous.[14] The figure for 19th century Constantinople was 2 percent. [15]

Mrs. Harvey, describes how some women, especially those from the royal family, prevented their husbands from marrying a second wife, citing several examples from Ottoman ladies she personally knew. Moreover, she also explains the financial reasons behind men's inability to marry more than one woman.

> Our friend, the hanoum, had been a well-portioned bride. She brought her husband, besides the house we had seen, another at Beyuk'dere, considerable property in land, and a large sum of money. Where a daughter is so richly dowered, the father usually stipulates that no other wife shall be taken. Wives also, in Constantinople, as elsewhere, are expensive luxuries, for each lady must have a separate establishment, besides retinue and carriage.[16]

Another misconception propagated by Western male travelers and adventurers is that harems were places where women congregated to allow their men to satiate their carnal desires.

---

[12] Julia Pardoe, p. 81.
[13] Harvey, p. 69.
[14] Philippe Fargues, "Family and Household in Mid-Nineteenth Century Cairo," Beshara Doumani (ed.), *Family History in the Middle East: Household, Property, and Gender*. New York: State University of New York Press, 2003, 23-51, p. 41
[15] Judith Tucker, "Ties That Bound: Women and Family in Eighteenth and Nineteenth Century Nablus," *Women in Middle Eastern History*. New York: Vail-Ballou Press, 1991, pp. 98, 233-254
[16] Harvey, *Turkish Harems and Circassian Homes*. London: Hurst and Blackett, 1871, p. 70

They maintained that the harem has no role pertaining to family and elderly women and children have no place there.

As can be seen from 19th century Western orientalist paintings, Western men saw harems as places where beautiful, half-naked women pranced around. Those who actually saw what took place in harems first hand objected to such characterization. Writers like Poole and Pardoe, who carefully observed the etiquette in harems, repeatedly affirmed that no immoral activities could be seen in harems.

> The ideas entertained by many in Europe of the immorality if the hareem are, I believe, erroneous.[17]

She saw harems as family institutions run in accordance with a strict moral code and, contrary to what Westerners thought, a system that allows women considerable freedom. When looked at from the outside, these two facts are not easy to see, she agrees, adding that while the harem system may seem to be based on contradictory principles, close inspection reveals that most women are happy and enjoy high standards of living.

> No person can imagine the strictness of the hareem without adopting its seclusion, nor can a stranger form a just estimate of the degree of liberty enjoyed by the women without mixing in Eastern society. One thing is certain, that if a husband is tyrant, his wife his slave; but such cases are extremely rare. I do not pretend to defend the system of marrying blindfold, as it were; nor do I look for those happy marriages which are most frequently found in England; but I am pleased to find the Eastern women contented, and without a single exception in my acquaintances, so cheerful that I naturally conclude that they are treated with consideration.[18]

Charles White, who lived in Constantinople in the 1840s,

---

[17] Sophia Lane-Poole, p. 137.
[18] Sophia Lane-Poole, p. 116.

wrote about how harems were family dwellings where virtue and ethics were of paramount importance. He also criticizes the dominant European fantasy about the sultan's harem. He argues that a single man's dominance over up to 350 women, most of whom selected for their beauty, may push one's imagination to the limits, but that the rules that dominate the harem restrain extreme actions.[19] He says that even if palace rules, coupled with religious and moral norms, do not dampen a man's appetites, women's jealousies surely will.[20]

In the part where he delves into the daily life in the sultan's harem, he says even the sultan is bound by the rules that govern harem.

Ottoman writer Halil Halid, who lived in Britain in the 19th century, in his book, *A Diary of a Turk*, says the image the harem produces in the West is mistaken and argues that the flawed perception is the reason behind the misrepresentation of Eastern women.

> There are many people in England whose ideas on the subject of the harem are but a confused misconception, based on what they may have heard about Eastern polygamy. In this chapter, that I may correct these mistaken conceptions, I will give some more exact information on the subject of the harem and its inmates, as well as on the position of women in Turkey in general. Although the word harem is known and used by the people of Western Europe, the true meaning of the term is understood by but few persons in this country. As a matter of fact, many subjects concerning the East are much misunderstood in the West, just as there are certain manners and customs of Western Europe that cause prejudice in the Eastern mind. When an Englishman uses the word harem,

---

[19] Charles White, p. 16.
[20] ibid., pp. 16-17.

he means thereby the numerous wives whom a man in our part of the East is supposed to shut up in his house. He, moreover, believes that every man in the Mohammedan East may marry as many women as he pleases. This idea is not only mistaken, but grotesque. There are thousands of men who would consider themselves fortunate if they could marry even a single woman; while, on the other hand, there are thousands who would be happy to get rid of the single wife they have. Any man who can manage to keep two, not to say more, wives in peace, and can cope with the requirements of each, must be an exceptionally brave person.[21]

Wives are not all religiously obedient in the East, just as all men are not tyrants. Religion, law, and custom impose upon men many duties to be discharged towards their wives. An honest man must discharge these duties, and indeed it is very difficult to find many men who are able to fulfil their obligations as husbands towards more than one wife. It has been proved that in many parts of the Ottoman empire the number of women does not exceed that of men, a fact which alone is enough to show the absurdity of the notion prevailing in England about the plurality of wives in that country.[22]

The writer then explains the falsehoods concerning the harem before describing the true purpose of the concept, as many Western women had done before him in their personal accounts. He says the harem is not a place where multiple women do the bidding of one man, but a family environment where female relatives and children live.

After pointing out the absurdity of the notion that a man's harem is his collection of wives, I will now explain what it really is. In Mohammedan countries, where the seclusion of women is a deeply rooted and religiously observed custom, every house is

---

[21] Halil Halid, pp. 46-49.
[22] ibid., pp. 46-49.

divided into two separate parts. In Turkey the section of a house where the ladies reside is called the harem, and the men's portion is named the selamlik — that is to say, the reception-place. Though the female inmates of a house are also collectively called the harem, this does not mean that they are all the wives of the master of the house. A man's wife, his mother, his sister, his daughter, and such other women as may lawfully appear unveiled in his presence, all belong to his harem.[23]

Mrs. Harvey, during her visit to Constantinople in late 19th century, said that an Ottoman pasha had to ask for his wife's permission to enter the harem and that all the women covered themselves out of respect before he entered the dwelling.

> During our visits to their wives the pashas often requested permission to enter the harem. It was sometimes amusing to see the astonishment of the women when they found we did not object to converse with the pasha. They could hardly understand that we would allow him to enter the harem during our stay there. In deference to their feelings we, however, always drew down our veils before the master of the house entered, a proceeding which we were aware materially increased their respect for us, and for our sentiments of reserve and propriety.[24]

Free Women of the Ottoman Empire

One interesting tradition almost every women traveler noted is usually depicted as a symbol of freedom for Ottoman women. Lady Montagu, Sophia Poole and Julia Pardoe say that the street shoes placed in front of the harem's door were to protect the lady's personal space. It meant that the woman was

---

[23] Halil Halid, p. 46-49.
[24] Harvey, p 92-93.

busy and wanted to be left alone. A husband who saw the shoes would not dare enter the harem and would wait in the selamlik until told otherwise. This symbolized what Pardoe described as men's respect for a woman's personal space, as well as the sanctity of the rules that governed the harem system. This tradition also belies the myth held among European men about the passionate women open to every sexual whim of their husband.

Pardoe, about the tradition, says:

> [I]t is also a fact that though a Turk has an undoubted right to enter the apartments of his wives at all hours, it is a privilege of which he rarely, I may almost say, never avails himself. One room in the harem is appropriated to the master of the house, and therein he awaits the appearance of the individual with whom he is summoned to his presence by a slave. Should he, on passing to his apartment, see sleepers at the foot of the stairs, he cannot, under any pretense, intrude himself in the harem: it is a liberty that every woman in the empire resent. When guests are on a visit for some days, he sends a slave forward to announce his approach, and thus gives them tome and opportunity to withdraw.[25]

Place of Women in 19th Century British and Ottoman Societies

The rights and freedoms enjoyed by Ottoman women surprised many Westerners at the time and spurred female travelers to often compare the two societies. Some Western women even used the status of Ottoman women to criticize the state of married women in their own societies.[26]

In 19th century Europe, the man of the house was the

---

[25] Julia Pardoe, pp. 96-97.
[26] Billie Melman discusses this issue in detail.

master, and the woman, upon marriage, immediately came under the absolute monetary and physical dominion of their husbands.[27] This is exactly why the slipper tradition of the harem, which demonstrated the respect shown to the privacy of Ottoman women, meant so much.

The feminist movement that grew by leaps and bounds in 19th century Western societies was a response to the status of women. For example, in 1929, famous writer Virginia Wolf, in her *A Room of One's Own*, argues that a woman who controls her domicile and money will be freer and more productive.

Joan Perkins, who studied 19th century women in Britain, describes marriage as a "gilded cage" for women.

No wonder Ottoman women's ability to define and protect their space against any encroachment of men so impressed Western women.[28] Orientalist narratives produce an image where Eastern women lay on the pillows all day doing nothing. This image produced by Western male travel writers was later backed by the orientalist paintings produced in the 19th century. The first-hand impressions produced by Western women debunked the men's claims about the daily lives of Ottoman women.

Edward Lane, who invited his sister to Cairo to indirectly gain access to the world of harems, explains what Eastern women did during the day.

> The care of their children is the primary occupation of the ladies of Egypt: they are also charged with the superintendence of domestic affairs; but, in most families, the husband alone at-

---

[27] Marilyn Yalom, *A History of the Wife*. New York: Harper Collins Publishers, 2001, pp. 135-140; Pat Jalland, *Women, Marriage and Politics 1860-1914*. Oxford: Oxford University Press, 1986, pp. 59-60.

[28] Joan Perkin, *Women and Marriage in Nineteenth Century England*. Chicago: Lyceum Books, 1989, p. 257.

tends to the household expenses. Their leisure hours are mostly spent in working with the needle; particularly in embroidering handkerchiefs, head-veils, &c, upon a frame called "menseg," with coloured silks and gold. Many women, even in the houses of the wealthy, replenish their private purses by ornamenting handkerchiefs and other things in this manner, and employing a "dellaleh" (or female broker) to take them to the market, or to other harems, for sale. The visit of one harem to another often occupies nearly a whole day. Eating, smoking, drinking coffee and sherbet, gossiping, and displaying their finery, are sufficient amusements to the company. On such occasions, the master of the house is never allowed to enter the harem, unless on some particular and unavoidable business ; and in this case, he must give notice of his approach, and let the visiters have sufficient time to veil themselves, or to retire to an adjoining room.

Being thus under no fear of his sudden intrusion, and being naturally of a lively and an unreserved disposition, they indulge in easy gaiety, and not unfrequently in youthful frolic. When their usual subjects of conversation are exhausted, sometimes one of the party entertains the rest with the recital of some wonderful or facetious tale. The Egyptian ladies are very seldom instructed either in music or dancing; but they take great delight in the performance...[29]

Harvey, too, emphasizes the dominance of Ottoman women in the management of the house.

A Turkish wife, whatever her rank, is always at home at sunset to receive her husband, and to present him with his pipe and slippers when, his daily work over, he comes to enjoy the repose of his harem. In most households also the wife superin-

---

[29] Edward Lane, pp. 194-195.

tends her husband's dinner, and has the entire control over all domestic affairs.[30]

Pardoe, on the other hand, succumbs to orientalist impressions while explaining how Ottoman women spent their days. She describes Eastern people as lazy and women of leading superfluously luxurious lives, adding that Ottoman women were free to visit their friends and go to public baths.

> [Y]ou hurry from the bed to the bath, whence you cannot possibly escape in less than two hours-and the business of the day is then generally terminated for a Turkish lady. All that remains to be done is to sit under the covering of the *tandour*, passing the beads of a perfumed chaplet rapidly through fingers—arranging and re-arranging the head-dress and ornaments—or put on the *yashmac* and *feridjhe*, and sally forth, accompanied by two or three slaves, to pay visits to favourite friends ; either on foot, in yellow boots reaching up to the swell of the leg, over which a slipper of the same colour is worn; or in an araba, our carriage of the country, all paint, gilding, and crimson cloth, nestled among cushions...[31]

From what Western female travelers wrote about Ottoman women's status at home and in the harem, we see that contrary to previously held beliefs, Ottoman women had considerable freedom in going outside their homes and were indeed not prisoners.[32] Travelogue writers also provide a detailed glimpse into the daily lives of women, discounting the oft-repeated Western myth that women were imprisoned in harems. Western men tried to portray Eastern women as caged birds imprisoned in their harems. For instance, when

---
[30] Harvey, p. 11.
[31] Pardoe, p. 31.
[32] For a detailed description on what Ottoman women did outdoors, see Fanny Davis, *Ottoman Lady*, pp. 144-145.

describing women in the sultan's harem, many describe them as "birds in the gilded prison." However, as the books written by female travelers make clear, Ottoman women were far from prisoners in harems.

Nineteenth century Ottoman women often visited their friends in other harems. Women from the lower classes often went shopping on their own. Many women spent their spare times at public entertainment centers.

William Thackeray, for example, references coming across woman buying shoes at covered bazaar in İzmir. He also writes about a group of women bargaining with a salesman for quite some time before deciding not to buy, and he cannot hide his surprise over the lack of any sign of anger in the salesman's face.

Many artists who lived for a time in the East often portrayed women on the streets in their paintings, prints and engravings. Thomas Allom, in his print dated 1839, *The Valley of Guiuk Suey, the Sweet Waters of Asia, on the Bosphorus*, depicts women going to a picnic with an ox drawn carriage in Küçüksu on the Anatolian side of Constantinople.

The women near a fountain, enjoying the nice weather and greenery while reclining on a kilim amid several street vendors.

Female travelers visiting harems wrote detailed descriptions of how they were treated, what they ate and drank and the rituals that accompanied everything. For example, just before food was presented, slave girls would bring a pitcher filled with water and a washbowl and pillows would be placed around the low table around which they would eat. Diners would wash up before and after the meal and were given embroidered towels to dry their hands.

After many visits to the harems of Ottoman pashas, Sophia Poole admits that it came natural for her to copy the manners that govern harems, adding how impressed she was with the hospitality she encountered.[33]

Poole and her brother Edward Lane, in addition to wearing local clothes, abided by the locals rules at home. In her book, Poole writes about how they adapted their dinning rules to Eastern customs.

> I think you would be amused could you see our dinner-arrangements at home. First, a small carpet is spread on the mat ; then, a stool cased with mother-of-pearl, &c. is placed upon it, and serves as the support of a round tray of tinned copper, on which is arranged our dinner, with a cake of bread for each person. A maid then brings a copper ewer and basin, and pours water on the hands of each of our party, and we arrange ourselves round the tray, our Eastern table-napkins spread on our knees. These are larger and longer than English hand-towels, that they may cover both knees when sitting in the Turkish manner.
>
> During the meal, the maid holds a water-bottle, or defends us from flies with a fly-whisk. Having no change of plates, knives, or forks, no time is lost at dinner.; and it usually occupies twenty minutes. Thus, much valuable One or two sweet dishes are placed on the tray with those which are savoury ; and it is singular to see the women of this country take morsels of sweet and savoury food almost alternately. Immediately after dinner, the ewer and basin are brought round, the stool and carpet are removed with the tray, and the stool is always placed in another room until again required. There is something very socia-

---

[33] Sophia Lane-Poole, p. 115.

ble in this mode of sitting at table, and it is surprising to see how many persons can sit with comfort round a comparatively small tray. I should advise you and other friends in England to resume the use of small round tables: I have often regretted they are no longer in fashion: for a small family, they are infinitely more comfortable than the large square or oblong tables used in England. Time is saved by avoiding works of supererogation.[34]

Female travelers, just like those in the pieces produced by Western painters, are interested in the outdoor activities of Ottoman women in Constantinople, with many writing long and detailed descriptions of what they saw.

While it is little more than a construction site nowadays, Julia Pardoe, who went on a picnic in Küçüksu with her father Major Thomas Pardoe, explains how enjoyable this popular excursion spot was at the time. Her account contradicts claims that women were not allowed outside in the Ottoman Empire, and rather describes how cosmopolitan 19th century Constantinople truly was.

> The Valley of Guiuk-Suy, thronged as I have attempted to describe it, presents a scene essentially Oriental in its character. The crimson covered carriages moving along beneath the trees — the white-veiled groups scattered over the fresh turf — the constant motion of the attendant slaves—the quaintly-dressed vendors of *mohalibè* and *sètèl* (or sweetmeats) moving; rapidly from point to point with their plateaux upon their heads, furnished with a raised shelf, on which the crystal or china plates destined to serve for the one, and the pink and yellow glories of the other, are temptingly displayed — the *yahourt*-merchant, with his yoke upon his shoulder, and his swinging trays cov-

---

[34] Sophia Lane-Poole, p. 115.

ered with little brown clay basins, showing forth the creamy whiteness of his merchandize—the vagrant exhibitors of dancing bears and grinning monkeys — the sunburnt Greek, with his large flapping hat of Leghorn straw, and Frank costume, hurrying along from group to group with his pails of ice ; and recommending his delicate and perishable luxury in as many languages as he is likely to earn piastres—the neverfailing water-carrier, with his large turban, his graceful jar of red earth, and his crystal goblet — the negroes of the higher harems, laden with carpets, chibouks, and refreshments for their mistresses—the fruit vendors, with their ruddy peaches, their clusters of purple grapes from Smyrna, their pyramidically-piled filberts, and their rich plums, clothed in bloom and gathered with their fresh leaves about them—the melon-merchants sitting among their upheaped riches ; the *pasteks* with their emerald-coloured rinds, and the musk-melons, looking like golden balls, and scenting the breeze as it sweeps over them ; the variety of costume exhibited by the natives, always most striking on the Asiatic shore— the ringing rattle of the tambourine, and the sharp wiry sound of the Turkish Zebec, accompanied by the shrill voices of half a dozen Greeks, seated in a semicircle in front of a beauty-laden araba—all combine to complete a picture so perfect of its kind, that, were an European to be transported to Guiuk-Suy, without any intermediate preparation, he would believe himself to be under the spell of an enchanter, and beholding the realization of what he had hitherto considered as the mere extravagance of some Eastern story-teller.[35]

Julia Pardoe also reminisces about the hospitality shown by Turkish women at Küçüksu picnics. Friendly Turkish women impressed her so much that she postulated that the reason why Ottoman and Western women fail to understand

---

[35] Pardoe, pp. 264-266.

each other is that they do not establish friendly relations. She explains her interactions with Turkish women as she was walking among groups of women with a friend of hers.

> I am obliged to concede that no assemblage of European gentlewomen would have welcomed among them two female strangers as the Turkish ladies, during the day which we spent at Guiuk-Suy, received my friend and myself. The wandering Giaours were everywhere greeted with smiles, urged to linger, invited to partake of every rural collation; treated, in short, as friends, rather than persons seen for the first, and, probably, the only time. And such a welcome as this might be secured by every Frank lady, did she consider it worth her while to conciliate the Turkish females, who are always sufficiently rewarded for their courtesy and kindness, by a gay smile and a ready acceptance of their proffered civility; and yet it is a singular fact, that the European ladies resident in Constantinople are scarcely acquainted with one Osmanli family, and have been asked more than once if I was not frightened of the Turkish women![36]

After a pleasant day spent in Küçüksu with groups of women, she criticizes the negative image of Turks in the West.

> I was never more struck with this truth than at Guiuk-Suy. I never saw the women of Turkey under a more favourable aspect. Every heart appeared to be holding holiday • and when, as evening closed, we returned to our caique, and bade adieu to the Valley of the Asian Sweet Waters, I felt that I knew them better—that I understood more correctly their social character than I had hitherto done; and it is an important fact, and one which is well worthy of remark, that the more a European, resolved to cast aside prejudice and to study the national habits and impuls-

[36] Pardoe, pp. 263-266.

es, comes in contact with the inhabitants of the East, the more he is led to admire the consistency of thought, feeling, and action which influence them, and the highminded generosity with which they tolerate the jarring and discordant habits and prejudices of their foreign visitors.[37]

Mrs. Harvey, who visited Constantinople 35 years after Julia Pardoe, in her 1871 book, *Turkish Harems and Circassian Homes*, includes a detailed description of Constantinople's women, especially their clothes, as they traveled to Küçüksu during religious holidays.

> Many a delightful hour did we pass in these valleys. The merry melodious voices of the women, the ringing laughter of the children, made a music very pleasant to the ear ; and the eye was charmed with the brilliant beauty of the colouring, and the picturesque grace of the groups that surrounded one on every side.
>
> On a Friday, or other holiday, many hundreds of people congregate at the Sweet Waters both of Europe and Asia. The women, arrayed in gorgeous dresses, recline on carpets beneath the trees, little spirals of smoke ascend from the numerous pipes, the narghile bubbles in its rose-water, the tiny cups of coffee send forth a delicious fragrance, the perfume of fresh oranges and lemons fills the air. The still more exquisite sweetness of orange blossoms is wafted towards us, as a gipsy flowergirl passes through the groups, carrying many a mysterious bouquet, of which the flowers tell a perhaps too sweet and too dangerous love-tale to the fair receiver.[38]

Another female travelogue writer Mrs. Hornby, who wrote about her years in Constantinople with her husband in *In and Around Stanboul*, provides an account of her impression of reli-

---

[37] Pardoe, p. 263.
[38] Harvey, p. 84-85.

gious holidays celebrated at Küçüksu and watching the bayram parade with a mixed group of men and women during the Crimean War (1853-1855). She also provides a glimpse into a time when Armenians, Greeks and Jews of the city joined their Muslim neighbors in the bayram celebrations.

Mrs. Hornby describes Küçüksu and the groups of men and women who went there to enjoy the religious holidays as well as women's dresses.

> The banks meanwhile are most lovely to look on. Your eye is charmed, delighted, and contented, for there is nothing to wish for, nothing to imagine: it is a full, complete, and harmonious picture. Here and there guitars hang on the trees. Group after group, in the most splendid and varied costumes, are seated under the dark plane trees, from their deepest shade down to the gay and sparkling water's edge, where a beauty in snow-white vail, and shining lilac feridjee trimmed with silver, is laughing with a lovely child and her black attendants, who are carrying embroidered cushions from the quietly moored caique. Every turn on the river brings you upon different groups on either side, the last appearing more striking than the first. By the landing-place the banks were literally lined with Turkish women in white vails, and feridjees of every possible brilliant or delicate color, from blue, trimmed with rose-color, and cherry trimmed with silver, to delicate apple-green and the palest strawcolor, The dark-brown and dark-green feridjees of the slaves, or the poorer women, prevent one's eye from being wearied with too much brilliancy. It is perfect, and you are delighted even with the rude Greek songs and their wiry-sounding guitars.[39]

In her book on life in Egypt at the time, Sophia Poole describes the Muslim women who travel alone in the city

---

[39] Hornby, pp. 372-376.

streets. As she walked along the street in front of Halile Khan, which was built by Ottoman sultans, she saw women riding donkeys, which she said was the perfect mode of transportation for women in the city.

> [W]e found ourselves in the main street of the city, opposite to the khan el- Khaleelee, the chief Turkish bazaar of Cairo. I felt more than ever convinced that donkeys were the only safe means of conveyance in the streets of this city. A lady never rides but on a donkey, with a small carpet laid over the saddle.[40]

Similarly, her brother Edward Lane, echoes Poole's impression that women usually prefered to ride donkeys in Egypt.

> Being raised so high above the back of the " homar 'alee " (or the " high ass "—for so the animal which they ride, furnished with the high saddle, is commonly called), they seem very insecurely seated; but I believe this is not really the case: the ass is well girthed, and sure-footed; and proceeds with a slow, ambling pace, and very easy motion. The ladies of the highest rank, as well as those of the middle classes, ride asses thus equipped : they are very seldom seen upon mules or horses. The asses are generally hired. When a lady cannot procure a homar 'alee, she rides one of the asses equipped for the use of the men; but has a " seggádeh (or prayer-carpet) placed over its saddle; and the inferior members of the hareem, and females of the middle orders, often do the same.[41]

Lane also explains how women on the streets did not walk if their destination was not near, and when they did walk, they pulled up the skirts of their dresses because of the difficulty of walking in the slippers they usually wore. He also

---
[40] Poole, p. 57.
[41] Lane, p. 196.

says men usually treated women riding donkeys on the streets with deference.

> Ladies never walk abroad, unless they have to go but a very short distance. They have a slow and shuffling gait, owing to the difficulty of retaining the slippers upon their feet ; and, in walking, they generally hold the front edges of the habarah in the manner represented in the engraving in page 47. Whether walking or riding, they are regarded with much respect in public : no well-bred man stares at them ; but rather directs his eyes another way. They are never seen abroad at night, if not compelled to go out or return at that time by some pressing and extraordinary necessity : it is their usual rule to return from paying a visit before sunset. The ladies of the higher orders never go to a shop, but send for whatever they want; and there are numerous dellalehs who have access to the hareems, and bring all kinds of ornaments, articles of female apparel, &c, for sale. Nor do these ladies, in general, visit.[42] (47)

Pardoe, meanwhile, says Turkish women in Constantinople can roam the city any way they want.

> "A Turkish woman consults no pleasure save her own when she wishes to walk or drive, or even to pass a short time with a friend; she adjusts her *yashmac* and *feridjhe*, summons her slave, who prepares her *boksha*, or bundle, neatly arranged in a muslin handkerchief; and, on the entrance of the husband, his inquires are answered by the intelligence that the Hanoum* Effendi is gone to spend a week at the harem of so and so. Should he be suspicious of the fact, he takes steps to ascertain that she is really there; but the idea of controlling her in the fancy, or of making it subject of reproach on her return, is perfectly out of the question."[43]

---

[42] ibid., p. 196.
[43] Pardoe, p. 97.

Hamam As Women's Coffee Shop

Apart from visiting regular excursion spots, attending circumcision and wedding ceremonies, and harem visits, the most important entertainment activity for Ottoman women outside their homes was going to hamams, or Turkish public baths. In Muslim societies, the special importance paid to the cleanliness of the body and clothes, and regular ablution, is naturally reflected also in most people's favorite pastimes. As one of the most favored spots in Ottoman cities, hamams also form a significant portion of what Western travelers wrote about Ottoman society.

Briton Will Seymour Monroe, for instance, in his 1907 book, *Turkey and the Turks*, wrote after a four-month visit to the Ottoman Empire in the early 1900s in which explains the importance Turks attach to cleanliness and bathing:

> With the Moslems cleanliness is not merely next to godliness, it is godliness. The Koran specifically enjoins regular and careful ablutions; and, in consequence, the Turks of Constantinople are said to be free from many of the physical ailments with which both the Christians and the Jews are habitually afflicted. Comparative immunity from disease, therefore, seems due to the large number and frequent use of Turkish baths. There are more than one hundred and thirty such baths at the capital. Every important mosque has its bath; and many of the mosque-baths have been endowed by philanthropic Moslems, so that the poor of the city may enjoy gratuitously the luxury of Turkish baths.[44]

Julia Pardoe one day went to a Turkish bath with her friends and wrote in detail about her experiences, the rules of the bath, the heat, the architecture and how the hamam worked:

> The process of Turkish bathing is tedious, exhausting, and trou-

---

[44] Will Seymour Monroe, *Turkey and the Turks*. Boston: Colonial Press, 1907, p. 227.

blesome; I believe that the pretty Greek who attended me spent an hour and a half over my hair alone. The supply of water is immense, and can be heated at the pleasure of the bather, as it falls into the marble basin from two pipes, the one pouring forth a hot, and the other a cold, stream. The marble on which you stand and sit is heated to a degree that you could not support, were the atmosphere less dense and oppressive ; and, as the water is poured over you from an embossed silver basin, the feeling of exhaustion becomes almost agreeable. Every lady carries with her all the appliances of the bath, as well as providing her own servant ; the inferior ranks alone availing themselves of the services of the bathing women, who, in such cases, supply their employers with everything requisite...

[T]he excessive exhaustion which it induces, and the great quantity of time which it consumes, are the only objections that can reason- ably be advanced against the use of the Turkish bath.[45]

Turkish baths also possessed a very social function in the lives of Ottoman women. Hamams, where women of all ages and social standing bathed, provided a public area where friends could meet and talk and where mothers on the lookout for brides for their sons could take an account of what was available.

Based on his observations of Ottoman Cairo, Edward Lane, describes women's visits to hamams:

Many persons go to the bath twice a week: others, once a week, or less frequently; but some are merely washed with soap and water, and then plunge into one of the tanks; for which, of course, they pay less. The women who can afford to do so visit the hammam frequently; but not so often as the men. When the bath is not hired for the females of one family, or for one

---

[45] Pardoe, p. 49.

> party of ladies, exclusively, women of all conditions are admitted. In general, all the females of a house, and the young boys, go together. They take with them their own seggidehs, and the napkins, basins, &c, which they require, and even the necessary quantity of sweet water for washing with soap, and for drinking; and some carry with them fruits, sweetmeats, and other refreshments.[46]

Lane also writes about how rich women hire special masseurs, and how the bath is a special meeting place for women of every social standing. There are always mothers looking for brides for their sons and women who want to show off their new jewelry.[47]

A century before them, Lady Montagu had realized the special function baths play in the social lives of Ottoman women.

> In short, 'tis the women's coffee house, where all the news of the town is told, scandal invented etc. They generally take this diversion once a week, and stay there at least four or five hours, without getting cold by immediate coming out of the hot bath into the cool room, which was very surprising to me.[48]

Julia Pardoe echoes Lady Montagu's description of Turkish baths as centers of social interactions for Ottoman women.

> I could form no adequate idea of what is understood by a Turkish bath; the terrestrial paradise of Eastern women, where politics, social and national, scandal, marriage, and every other subject under heaven, within the capacity of uneducated but quick-witted females, is discussed: and where ample revenge is

---

[46] Lane, p. 349.
[47] ibid., p. 349.
[48] Montagu, p. 70.

taken for the quiet and seclusion of the harem, in the noise, and harry, and excitement, of a crowd.[49]

In the context of what Western women wrote about Ottoman women and the daily lives of their British counterparts, it would not be too hyperbolic to say that apart from minor discrepancies, the lives of Ottoman and British women at home and on the street were remarkably similar.

Both societies opposed the employment of women from the middle and upper classes and, consequently, working women were habitually from the lower classes.[50] During the reign of Queen Victoria (1837-1901), the usual activities of women with middle class backgrounds were limited to going to church, philanthropic visits to the poor, and getting together with friends.[51] The most popular hobby pursued at home was knitting and sewing. British women, unlike Ottoman women, were also very well read. Writing letters to friends and family was a favorite pastime.

Aristocratic women, as opposed to the more traditional and religious women of the bourgeoisie, spent most of their time dancing at balls, gambling, and showing off their dresses.[52] They used their own vehicles to visit friends or go shopping, while women from the bourgeoisie usually used public transportation.

As the train network developed in the decades following the 1830s, women from both aristocratic and bourgeois backgrounds found the opportunity to travel much further than before, some even venturing overseas. While the most popular destinations

---

[49] Pardoe, p.47.
[50] Tucker, p. 79.
[51] Yalom, p. 181.
[52] Joan Perkin, *Victorian Women*. New York: New York University Press, 1993, pp. 93-94, 98-102

were France and Germany due to proximity, a considerable minority traveled to the lands of the Ottoman Empire.[53]

Status of Ottoman Women in the Eyes of Travelers

Apart from describing how Ottoman women lived at home and outside, Western travelers were particularly interested in the marriage and divorce rights of Ottoman women, who mostly enjoyed greater rights than their European counterparts. Concerning the right to divorce, marry, purchase property, and custody of children, Ottoman women clearly had more inalienable rights than women in Europe. Comparative analyses in the section, too, are based on the observations of Western travelers and academic studies.

There are obvious differences between the Western and Ottoman institutions of family, marriage, and women's rights. The most important disparity involves the financial status of women before, during, and after marriage. According to Islamic canon law, or *fiqh*, a woman's property does not transfer to her husband upon marriage. She has absolute control over the money and financial assets she brought to the marriage and her husband cannot use or control her property without her explicit permission.

Islamic law allows individuals' acquisition of property. In other words, it allows and protects personal property. Any assault on an individual's property is one of the worst sins, and also has legal repercussions.

Additionally, men have the legal obligation to cover their wives' material expenses. Such financial advantages allowed rich Muslim women to establish charitable founda-

[53] ibid., p. 102.

tions, or *waqf*, and donate their time and money to establishing mosques, fountains, or other charitable endeavors.[54] One striking example is the many architectural masterpieces endowed by female members of the Ottoman royal family.

Ottoman society researcher Judith Tucker, in her article "The Middle East and North Africa: The 19th and 20th Centuries," argues that the fact that upper class Ottoman women lived in harems did not necessarily mean that they were not an integral part of economic life. She explains that women usually hired intermediaries to manage foundation affairs and played a key part in economic activity in the Ottoman Empire.

She explains that women from the upper classes played a central part in metropolitan economies from the 16th to and 19th century, and adds that, as members of rich and influential families, they also owned a considerable amount of property. Studies focusing on sale transactions of land, activities of foundations, plot allotments, and court records confirm this. Female members of the Ottoman upper classes had extensive properties and great financial clout. Their personal control over inheritance and wedding gifts is evidence that their legal sway was no coincidence. [55]

Many historians who study Ottoman society affirm that women owned between one-third to half of all foundations established in the main metropolitan centers of the Ottoman Empire in the 19th century, such as Damascus, Cairo, and Constantinople.[56]

Tucker cites that women commissioned or renovated 33 mosques in Constantinople in the 18th and 19th centuries.[57]

---

[54] For detailed information, see Tucker, p. 81.
[55] Tucker, p. 80.
[56] ibid., p. 81.
[57] ibid., p. 93.

According to a 1930 study, of the 491 fountains in Istanbul, women commissioned 128.[58]

In her article "Women, Law and Imperial Justice", after a detailed study of complaints submitted to the Divan-ı Hümayun, which approximately corresponds to today's ministerial cabinet, Fariba Zarinebaf-Shahr describes how women were economically prominent in the 17th and 18th centuries and represented themselves at court.[59] Court ledgers show that most of women's wealth came from inheritance, wedding presents, and dowries, and both married and single women had the right to manage their wealth. Studies show that women used their accumulated wealth for commercial enterprises and property purchases.[60]

Women who objected to local court decisions often took their cases to the Divan-ı Hümayun in Constantinople, and as records show, many did. For example, between 1680 and 1706, 8.4 percent of all complaints to the Divan-ı Hümayun came from women.[61] This rate rises considerably for local courts concerning issues of inheritance and wedding presents. In the province of Kayseri, between 1590 and 1630, 25 percent of all plaintiffs were women in cases submitted to the court and overseen by the local *qadi*, or governor.[62]

According to Jennings' studies conducted, two of the six court cases at a local Kayseri court on Rajab 22, 1027 of the Is-

---

[58] Fanny Davis, *The Ottoman Lady: A Social History from 1718 to 1918*. New York: Greenwood Press, 1986, p. 218.
[59] Fariba Zarinebaf-Shahr, "Women, Law, and Imperial Justice in Ottoman Istanbul in the Late Seventeenth Century," *Women, the Family, and Divorce Laws in Islamic History*, Amira El Azhary Sonbol (ed.). Syracuse: Syracuse University Press, 1996, pp. 81-95
[60] Zarinebaf-Shahr, p. 94.
[61] ibid., p. 86.
[62] ibid., p. 86; Ronald C. Jennings, *Women in Early 17th Century Ottoman Judicial Records: The Sharia Court of Anatolian Kayseri, Journal of the Economic and Social History of the Orien*. vol. 18, No. 1 (Jan. 1975), pp. 53-114, 59.

lamic calendar (July 15, 1618) involved women.[63] Jennings also notes that women had equal rights to men in filing at courts, and sharia courts specially protected women. Such studies demonstrate that concerning representing themselves and filing complaints, women enjoyed equal rights before the law.

Origins of Women's Rights in the Ottoman Empire

Women's property rights in the Ottoman Empire were based on clear Islamic precedents. The women of Prophet Muhammad's family also engaged in commercial activities in the first years of Islam. That era also saw women employed in various capacities, and even engaging in martial activities from time to time. The prophet's first wife Khadija bint Khuwaylid, before marrying him, was engaged in trade, personally managing caravan trade in Mecca. Her job would correspond somewhat to the CEO of a modern export-import company. The prophet's fifth wife, Zaynab bint Khuzayma, gave alms from the money she earned. Another of the prophet's wives, Aisha bint Abi Bakr, speaking about Zaynab, said, "The most generous amongst us is Zaynab, because, she works, and gives alms from her earnings."[64] There were many female executives in Islamic history. For instance, Islam's first nurse, Rufaida al-Aslamia, managed a nursing home.[65], [66] Caliph Omar even appointed al-Shifa' bint Abdullah as the manager of a bazaar in Medina.[67]

When the Mamluks ruled Egypt in the 13th century,

---

[63] Jennings, p. 58.
[64] Hadith cited by Abu Muslim.
[65] Mohammad Ali Syed, *The Position of Women in Islam: A Progressive View*, Albany: State University of New York Press, 2004, p. 26.
[66] Amina Wadud, "The Koran Teaches that Women Have the Same Rights as Men", Margaet Speaker Yuan (ed.), *Women in Islam*. Detroit: Greenhaven Press, 2005, p. 9-14, p. 11.
[67] al-Khalaf, Moodhy, "Islamic Tradition Proves that the Women Have the Right to Be Leaders", Margaret Speaker Yuan (ed.), *Women in Islam*. Detroit: Greenhaven Press, 2005, p. 29-34. p. 33.

women founded and to some extent managed five madrasahs.[68] Women took up important posts during and after the prophet's lifetime. Caliph Abu Bakr, when the Quran was compiled in book form, Omar's daughter Hafsa was given the duty to protect and memorize the holy book. Along with Aisha, she was one of the principle narrators of hadiths.[69]

Women played an important part in education, as well. It is said that Andalusian scholar Ibn Arabi's two most important teachers were women. In turn, Ibn Arabi educated his own daughter, who was able to answer complicated theological questions at a very early age.[70]

Another important female figure in Islamic history is the poet Rabi'a al-'Adawiyya al-Qaysiyya, or Rabia of Basra, who lived in the ninth century in Basra and became a very important figure in Sufi tradition.[71]

Ottoman women from wealthy families were trained in calligraphy, continuing the tradition of educated women in Islamic history. For instance, Feride Hanım and Ermine Servet Hanım were famous 19th century calligraphers.[72]

Advancement of Women's Rights in Europe

Women's rights and freedoms were protected and preserved in Islamic and Ottoman, societies, while from the Middle Ages, when Christianity started to become institutionalized in Europe, until the late 19th century, British women, when they married,

---

[68] Jonathan P.Berkey,, "Women and Islamic Education in the Mamluk Period", *Women in Middle Eastern History*. New York: Vail-Ballou Press, 1991, pp. 143-161, 144.
[69] Seyd pp. 25-26.
[70] Leila Ahmed, "Early Islam and the Position of Women: The Problem of Interpretation," *Women in Middle Eastern History*. New York: Vail-Ballou Press, 1991, pp. 58-74, 69.
[71] ibid., p. 58-74, 67.
[72] Tucker, p. 94; Davis, p. 227.

were not seen as a separate individual from their husbands before the law. The personal rights of women were transferred to their husbands upon marriage, with the consequent results that naturally infuriated 19th century feminists, as explained below.

Joan Perkin, in her book *Women and Marriage in Nineteenth Century England*, explains:

> A man and wife were one person in law; her existence was, as it were, absorbed in that of her husband; she lived under his protection or cover, and her condition was called coverture.[73]

Mary Lyndon Shanley, in *Feminism, Marriage and the Law in Victorian*, argues that feminists saw marriage as synonymous to slavery because as per common law, a woman was basically the property of her husband. The principle of coverture made it mandatory for a woman's legal existence to come under her husband's dominion upon marriage.[74]

This law was based on William Blackstone's book *Commentaries of the Laws of England (1765-1769)*. According to Backstone, upon marriage, all legal rights of women belong to their husbands, and that if man and wife are of one body before God, so must it be before the law. And according to law, it is the man who represents this joint body. [75]

As a consequence, a married woman in the West had no authority to sign any legal contract without the consent of her husband. A woman's paramount duty was to accept the man as the master of the house and obey his commands.[76] Middle and upper class families frowned upon the employment of women in any

---

[73] Perkin, *Victorian Women*, p. 13.
[74] Mary Lyndon Shanley, *Feminism, Marriage and the Law in Victorian England*. New Jersey: Princeton University Press, 1989, p. 8.
[75] ibid. p. 8; Yalom, p. 185; Levine, Philippa, *Victorian Feminism 1850-1900*, Tallahassee: The Florida State University Press, 1987, p. 134.
[76] Perkin, *Victorian Women*.

capacity apart from those relevant to child rearing. In Britain, a woman's responsibilities could be summarized as obeying one's husband, keeping the house clean, and raising the children.[77]

Until 1884, a married British woman's status before the law was as chattel, the dictionary meaning of which is "slave" or "property".

In her 1989 book *Feminism Marriage and the Law in Victorian England* Shanley explains how 19th century women's rights activists criticized women's status before the law, describing how women lost almost all legal rights enjoyed by single men and women once married.[78] Losing rights upon marriage also had significant practical consequences, among which were the loss of legal right to sign documents and the legal right to represent oneself. Married women could not file a complaint, nor could they be charged unless accused of murder or treason.

For instance, only a woman's husband could lodge a complaint if she was the victim of an offense. If a woman wanted to file a complaint, she had to get her husband's approval.[79]

The concept of coverture in British common law also took away married women's property rights. A single woman was seen as an individual before the law and could purchase and control her assets, but once married, she lost control over her assets to her husband. The control of properties brought to the household by the wife was immediately transferred to the husband.[80] Again, Perkin explains the law of coverture:

> A wife's personal property before marriage (such as stock, shares, money in hand, money at the bank, jewels, household

---

[77] Yalom, p. 181.
[78] Shanley, p. 10.
[79] Yalom, p. 139.
[80] Yalom, p. 139.

goods, clothes, etc.), though not her freehold land, became her husband's absolutely, unless settled in trust for her. The husband could assign or dispose of it at his pleasure, whether he and his wife lived together or not.[81]

In other words, before the legislations passed between 1870 and 1882, a woman's property, which she usually inherited from her family, was passed to her husband upon marriage. A woman had no right to use the property.[82] A husband could do with his wife's property anything he deemed fit. He had to leave one-third of it to his wife upon his death, but the rest he could be dispersed without any legal restraint.[83]

Under certain conditions, husbands could even violate this rule and leave their wife nothing whatsoever. For example, a woman from northern Britain opened a hat shop after her husband went bankrupt. The money she earned not only covered the household's upkeep, but also created a small fortune for the family. However, the man, in his will, left everything to his illegitimate children, leaving the woman penniless upon his death.[84]

Courts registered women's stolen or missing property as belonging to their husbands because married women could not legally own property.[85] Two examples Perkin cites in *Victorian Women* show that two women whose purses were stolen joined the women's freedom movement to get this law annulled. Harriet Grote, who was the wife of a banker/historian, had her watch and purse stolen. When she went to court, she was surprised that the stolen property was registered as

---

[81] Perkin, *Victorian Women*, p. 13.
[82] Rachel G. Fuchs, and Victoria E. Thompson, *Women in Nineteenth Century Europe*. New York: Palgrave Macmillan, 2005, p. 53.
[83] Yalom, p. 185.
[84] Perkin, *Victorian Women*, p. 89.
[85] ibid., p. 14.

belonging to her husband, which led her to do something to change it. Millicent Garrett Fawcett, who was the wife of an MP, also had her purse stolen in the 1870s. She argued that when her purse was registered as her husbands, she felt as if she was being accused of theft, and eventually became one of the leading members of the British feminist movement.[86] In time, the women's rights movement fittingly criticized the fact that married women's status was akin to that of children.

Women of the aristocracy, thanks to their wealth, were not bound by the limitations imposed on the women of the bourgeoisie and working class. When their daughters got married, many aristocratic fathers opened trust accounts in their name, preventing their husband from having complete financial domination over them. This tradition, however, was true for a small minority, not for the lower classes and bourgeoisie, whose women continued to be victimized by the law.[87]

Another example is Nelly Weeton, who married Aaron Stock in 1814. Before her marriage, Weeton was working as a governess, which was the most common job for a single, middle-class woman of the time, and with the money she earned, had purchased a village house. However, only a few years after they were married, Stock started to leave her without any money when angry, according to Weeton's diary. Weeton also complained about her husband's absolute control over her hard-earned money and home. As the relationship deteriorated even further, Stock gave control of the household to his daughter from a different woman and threatened to evict his wife. He also accused her of assault, resulting in her arrest. She finally had enough, and got a document of separation in 1820, as divorce was illegal at the time. The court awarded

---

[86] ibid., p. 89.
[87] ibid., p. 76.

her only 50 of the 75 pounds of revenue from her house. On top of all of it, she was prevented from seeing her children for many years, as they were legally their father's wards.[88]

Injustice faced by married women was not limited to ordinary citizens. For instance, famous writer Elizabeth Gaskell accused her husband of enriching himself with the money she earned. Another female writer, Charlotte Elizabeth Phelan, born in 1790, wrote about how the husband she separated from tried to seize the money she earned. She even sued him to keep her own money.[89]

Money earned by married women automatically became the property of the husband. In other words, women had no say over the money they earned. Their payroll had no legal admissibility. Anytime he wanted, the husband could seize the wife's salary.[90] The following is an often-cited example. A British woman established a public laundry after her husband left her. Her business took off and she deposited all the money she made in a bank. Her missing husband, after learning his wife is now rich, returned and seized the money in the bank because it legally belonged to him.[91]

In her book, Marilyn Yalom says that a man who gets married in church promises to bestow on his wife all his worldly possessions, but in practice, a woman's property belongs to the husband.[92]

Despite all the disadvantages, only one in six women in 19th century Britain remained unmarried.[93] Experts be-

---

[88] ibid., p. 114.
[89] ibid., p. 90.
[90] Perkin, *Women and Marriage in Nineteenth Century England*. p. 14.
[91] Perkin, *Victorian Women*, p. 89.
[92] Yalom, p. 74.
[93] Kathryn Gleadle, *British Women in the Nineteenth Century*. New York: Palgrave, 2001, p. 183.

lieve social isolation, the hardships faced by so-called spinsters, along with being forced to be dependent on relatives in old age, prevented many from eschewing marriage.[94] That is why, despite all the problems associated with it, marriage was a necessity for women in the Victorian age.[95]

These difficulties acted as a spark in the emergence of the feminist movements defending women's rights in the West. Mary Wollstonecraft, who lived in the 18th century, was one such pioneer.[96]

Another feminist pioneer, Barbara Leigh Smith Bodichon, wrote an article criticizing the many difficulties women faced in 1854, which had an enormous influence on the women's movement. The article, accompanied by a petition with 3,000 signatures, was submitted to British Parliament in 1856, calling for the reinstitution of women's right to own and control their own properties. These women's activism had a pronounced effect on the speedy passage of the Divorce Act in 1857.[97]

While incremental improvements were seen throughout the 19th century, until the passage of the 1870 and 1882 Married Woman's Property Act toward the end of the century, women continued to be victimized by their husbands. A married woman won the right to own and control her own property only after 1882.[98]

In most Muslim areas, including the Ottoman Empire, assets remained under the control of women before and during marriage – a right British women won only in 1882. The same law also conferred on British women the legal right to file

---

[94] Jalland, p. 79.
[95] Perkin, *Victorian Women*, p. 75.
[96] Yalom, pp. 74-75; Perkin, *Victorian Women*. p. 90; Perkin, *Women and Marriage in Nineteenth Century England*. p. 2.
[97] Philippa Levine, *Victorian Feminism 1850-1900*. Tallahassee: The Florida State University Press, 1987, p. 135-136.
[98] Fuchs, Rachel G. and Victoria E. Thompson, p. 53.

complaints, sign legal documents, and control assets. With the same law, women earned the right to demand during divorce proceedings all their assets earned before marriage.[99]

The Turkish common law instituted after the founding of the Republic in 1923 was based on Swiss common law, which granted married women the right to control their own assets only in 1874.[100] Married French women, in accordance with the 213th section of French common law, had no right to control their own property until the end of the 19th century. Women were under the total dominion of men, whose orders they had to obey no matter what. Women's property was under the total control of their husbands in France and Switzerland, just like in Britain. Children were the wards of their fathers and mothers had no say. In certain regions of Germany, women's lot was somewhat better than in Britain. Some German women were allowed control of the money they earned.[101]

It took feminists decades of activism for British Parliament to pass the acts of 1872 and 1882 that granted women the right to control their own personal matters. Conservative Christian groups condemned the passage of these laws, arguing that the economic independence accorded to women would eventually make them lose their way.

Conservative MP Henry Raikes argued that the act would allow women during arguments to threaten to leave their husbands and move in with someone who loved them better. He also claimed that giving women the right to control their own assets would create an abnormal, unnatural, and unbalanced equality between genders.[102]

Feminist and women's rights pioneer Barbara Leigh Smith

---

[99] Yalom, p. 189.
[100] ibid., p. 264.
[101] Rachel G. Fuchs, and Victoria E. Thompson, p. 53.
[102] Yalom p. 189

Bodichon attracted significant ire form conservatives due to the campaigns she initiated in the 1850s. Even the British media criticized her calls for women to have the right to manage their own fortunes as selfish and damaging to the sanctity of marriage.[103] One respected British newspaper, the Saturday Review, described those who campaigned for women's property rights as disease ridden. Until 1896, women never had control of the division of assets.[104]

Women's Rights in the Ottoman Empire

Despite problems in practice, the institution of marriage in Ottoman society aimed to protect the rights of both parties. Contrary to what was taking place in Italy, Britain, France, and other Western countries and empires, and even colonial India, Ottoman laws protected the financial rights of married women. Husbands were obligated to financially support their wives. In Italy, one fact that remained fixed since the Middle Ages was that a father had to start saving for a dowry the moment his daughter was born. There were even savings funds for dowries called *Monte delle doti* in Florence. The dowry the father of the bride would give to the groom was usually spent for the couple to begin their new lives. The amount of the dowry was seen as revealing the worth of the bride's family.[105] In Britain, too, it was the bride's father who was obligated to provide funds for the new couple to begin their married life.[106]

In Ottoman society, and according to Islamic law, wedding presents, or *mihr*, were defined as the presents that the

---

[103] Perkin, Victorian Women, p. 91.
[104] ibid., p. 92.
[105] Yalom, p. 85.
[106] Jalland, p. 58.

groom's family were obligated to give to the bride, which she was free to dispose of in accordance with her wishes.[107] Quranic verses on marriage set *mihr* as one of the prerequisites for the marriage to be religiously sanctified. [108], [109]

Abdal-Rehim cites the example of a marriage contract signed by a woman from the Hanafi school of Islam in front of a *qadi* in an article about marriage and family in Egypt. According to the contract, Omar, son of Muhammad, agreed to hand over three gold Maghreb dinars upfront to Zaynab, daughter of Abdullah, before marriage as part of the agreed five Maghreb dinar wedding gift. He also agreed to give three gold Maghreb dinars if he were to die or divorce the woman. The marriage contract also includes the husband's payment of half a silver Suleymaniya dinar to the wife to cover monthly expenses. Omar also agreed to his wife's right to divorce through *talakh* if he makes her to move elsewhere without her consent, marries a second woman, or mistreats her.[110]

Another woman received 25 golden Sultani dinars upon marriage and five dinars in installments over 20 years.[111]

Fanny Davis says *mihr*, or wedding gifts, were divided into two categories in Ottoman society. One was the amount paid before marriage to cover house and wedding costs. In

---

[107] O. Spies, "Mehr" *Islam Encyclopedia, v. VII.* Istanbul: M. E. B., 1979, p. 494.
[108] Also (forbidden are) women already married, except those (captives and slaves) whom your right hands possess. Thus has Allah ordained for you. All others are lawful, provided you seek (them in marriage) with Mahr (bridal money given by the husband to his wife at the time of marriage) from your property, desiring chastity, not committing illegal sexual intercourse, so with those of whom you have enjoyed sexual relations, give them their Mahr as prescribed; but if after a Mahr is prescribed, you agree mutually (to give more), there is no sin on you. Surely, Allah is Ever All-Knowing, All-Wise. Quran 4:24
[109] Seyd, pp. 91-94; Davis, p. 65; Quranic verses on *mihr*: 4:34, 2:241.
[110] Abdal-Rehim Abdal-Rahman Abdal-Rehim, "The Family and Gender Laws in Egypt During the Ottoman Period," Amira El Azhary Sonbol (ed.), *Women, the Family, and Divorce Laws in Islamic History.* Syracuse: Syracuse University Press, 1996, pp. 96-111, 98.
[111] Abdal-Rehim, p. 102.

the 19th century, this amounted to between 5,000 and 20,000 golden coins. The second category was the amount the husband promises his wife if they divorce. The same amount was the wife's right if the husband died while married.[112]

Professor of Arabic Edward Lane, who lived in Cairo between 1825 and 1845, in his book, *Manners and Customs of the Modern Egyptians*, explains how marriage among Muslims is conducted. He mentions the obligatory *mahr*, which he describes as a security payment for women. He refers to the relevant verse in the Quran, noting the fact Muslim women had the right to conduct all sorts of property transactions before, during, and after marriage.

> Whatever property the wife receives from her husband, parents, or any other person, is entirely at her won disposal and not subject to any claim of her husband or his creditors.[113]

The amount of money paid depended on the youth, beauty, and qualities of the bride, the family history, whether she was divorced or not, and the financial state of the groom. Still, sharia courts set the minimum amount to be paid at 10 dirhams. Lane cites the same figure in his book.

> The marriage of a man and woman, or of a man and a girl who has arrived at puberty, is lawfully effected by their declaring (which the latter generally does by a "wekeel," or deputy) their consent to marry each other, in the presence of two witnesses (if witnesses can be procured), and by the payment, or part-pay rent, of a dowry. But the consent of a girl under the age of puberty is not required; her father, or, if he be dead, her nearest adult male relation, or any person appointed as her guardian by will or by the Kadeem, acting for her as he pleases. The giv-

---

[112] Davis, p. 65.
[113] Lane, p. 101.

ing of a dowry is indispensable, and the least sum that is allowed by law is ten "dirhems," (or drachms or silver), which is equal to about five shillings of our money. A man may legally marry a woman without mentioning a dowry; but after the consummation of the marriage she can, in this case, compel him to pay the sum of ten dirhems.[114]

In certain cases, Ottoman law allowed the payment of *mihr* with property. According to a registry from Bursa, a man who worked as a porter married a slave he freed and gave his home, garden, and an additional 100 dirhams as *mihr*.[115]

Divorce Law

In addition to writing about marriage and other social interactions, Western travelers often commented on divorce and what happened to women afterward. One fact that surprised them the most was that divorce was allowed in the Ottoman Empire under certain conditions while it was totally banned in Europe.[116]

As mentioned in the hadiths, while frowned upon, divorce was a right granted to both men and women. "For Allah, divorce is the ugliest thing among that which is halal."[117]

---

[114] Lane, p. 101.
[115] Saadet Maydaer, "Ways for women to earn a fortune in the classical Ottoman era – The Bursa example," *Uludağ University Faculty of Theology Journa.*, Bursa, 2006, v:15, number 2, pp. 365-381.
[116] O Prophet! When you divorce women, divorce them at their *'iddah* (prescribed periods), and count (accurately) their *'iddah* (periods). And fear Allah your Lord (O Muslims), and turn them not out of their (husband's) homes, nor shall they (themselves) leave, except in case they are guilty of some open illegal sexual intercourse. And those are the set limits of Allah. And whosoever transgresses the set limits of Allah, then indeed he has wronged himself. You (the one who divorces his wife) know not, it may be that Allah will afterward bring some new thing to pass (i.e., to return her back to you if that was the first or second divorce). Quran 65:1-2
[117] Hadith from Abu Davud, Muhammed Seyd, p. 59.

This is why it is said everything possible should be done to reconcile husband and wife. Divorce has always been allowed under certain conditions in Islamic law.[118]

Lane gives a detailed description of the divorce process in the Ottoman Empire.

> A man may divorce his wife twice, and each time take her back without any ceremony, except in a case to be mentioned below, but if he divorce her the third time, or put her away by a triple divorce conveyed in one sentence, he cannot receive her again until she has been married and divorced by another husband, who must have consummated his marriage with her. When a man divorces his wife (which he does by merely saying, "Thou art divorced," or "I divorce thee"), he pays her a portion of her dowry (generally one-third), which he had kept back from the first, to be paid on this occasion or at his death; and she takes away with her the furniture, &c, which she brought at her marriage.[119]

In the 19th century, men utilized their right to divorce while women applied to courts for the same thing. There were also cases in which men agreed in pre-marriage contracts on their wives' right to divorce without going to court.[120]

In the travel book he published in 1845, Charles White describes Ottoman women's right to seek divorce according to his observations during his three years in Constantinople. He says this right is supported and protected by the sultan

---

[118] If you fear a breach between them twain (the man and his wife), appoint (two) arbitrators, one from his family and the other from hers; if they both wish for peace, Allah will cause their reconciliation. Indeed Allah is Ever All-Knower, Well-Acquainted with all things. (Koran 4:35) And if a woman fears cruelty or desertion on her husband's part, there is no sin on them both if they make terms of peace between themselves; and making peace is better. And human inner-selves are swayed by greed. But if you do good and keep away from evil, verily, Allah is Ever Well-Acquainted with what you do. Quran 4:28
[119] Lane, p. 101-102.
[120] Syed, p. 70.

himself. He also mentions that while allowed, polygamy, as the Quran dictates, needs to be based on justice and equality between men and women.

While allowing men to marry more than one woman, the Quran stipulates that marriage rights be divided equally between husband and wife. Women have the right to apply to court for divorce if their husbands neglect them. Courts always take up such applications and these women could always count of their family's support. Even the sultan would respect court decisions in such private cases.[121]

Sophia Poole, wrote in the early 19th century about how women in Egypt could apply to courts for divorce and other financial issues.

> There are five minor courts of justice in Cairo ; and likewise one at its principal port, Boolak; and one at its southern port, Masr El-'Ateekah. A deputy of the chief Kádee presides at each of them, and confirms their acts. The matters submitted to these minor tribunals are chiefly respecting the sales of property, and legacies, marriages, and divorces; for the Kádee marries female orphans under age who have no relations of age to act as their guardians; and wives

> often have recourse to law to compel their husbands to divorce them. In every country town there is also a Kádee, generally a native of the place, but never a Turk, who decides all cases, sometimes from his own knowledge of the law, but commonly on the authority of a Muftee.

> One Kádee generally serves for two or three or more villages.[122]

While some female travelers criticized the ease with which

---

[121] Charles White, p. 8.
[122] Poole, Appendix, p. 235.

divorce took place in Ottoman society in comparison to their own, many more praised the system. One aspect that garnered significant praise was the way Ottoman women were assured economic safety after divorce. In Britain, divorce usually took place when husbands deserted their wives, and due to significant obstacles preventing divorce, women were deprived of some of their rights. Most cases ended with women being penniless.[123]

As many travelers mentioned, men in Ottoman society had to live apart for approximately three to four months without any sexual relations with their ex-wives after divorce in order to ensure the woman was not pregnant, while maintaining them economically.[124]

Lane explains the process:

The "'eddeh" is the period during which a divorced woman, or a widow, must wait before marrying again; in either case, if pregnant, until delivery: otherwise, the former must wait three lunar periods, or three months; the latter four-months and ten days. The man who divorces his wife must maintain her in his own house, or in that of her parents, or elsewhere, during the period of her 'eddeh; but must cease to live with her as her husband from the commencement of that period.[125]

Moreover, a divorcing husband needed to pay his wife the

---

[123] Perkin.
[124] Relevant Quranic verses: 2:241: And for divorced women, maintenance (should be provided) on reasonable (scale). This is a duty on Al-Muttaqun (the pious). 65:6: Lodge them (the divorced women) where you dwell, according to your means, and do not treat them in such a harmful way that they be obliged to leave. And if they are pregnant, then spend on them till they deliver. Then if they give suck to the children for you, give them their due payment, and let each of you accept the advice of the other in a just way. But if you make difficulties for one another, then some other woman may give suck for him (the father of the child). 65: 7: Let the rich man spend according to his means, and the man whose resources are restricted, let him spend according to what Allah has given him. Allah puts no burden on any person beyond what He has given him. Allah will grant after hardship, ease.
[125] Lane, pp. 101-102.

amount of *mihr* he promised before marriage for the woman's economic security. For example, in Bursa's 19th century court registry, a man paid his *mihr* debt of 10,000 coins with a house worth 13,500 coins.[126]

Additionally, many female travelers were surprised that divorce in Ottoman society was seen as a temporary affair for women and was not associated with any discrimination. Divorce did not harm a woman's honor, nor did it affect her lifestyle that much. Women were not forced to vacate their homes. For instance, Lady Montagu, who lived with her husband in Constantinople in the 18th century, praises the economic independence of Ottoman women even after they are divorced.

> Neither have they much to apprehend from the resentment of their husbands, those ladies that are rich having all their money in their own hands. Upon the whole, I look upon the Turkish women as the only free people in the empire ; the divan pays a respect to them ; and the grand signior himself, when a pacha is executed, never violates the privileges of the haram (or women's apartment), which remains unsearched and entire to the widow.[127]

On the other hand, divorce or widowhood meant unfortunate consequences for British women. Until mid-19th century, widows could not attend entertainment activities nor could they go shopping, unlike their married counterparts. Widowhood meant emotional and financial ruin most of the time.[128] While middle-class women did not have the right to take over their husbands' businesses, it was somewhat easi-

---

[126] Saadet Maydaer, "Ways for women to earn a fortune in the classical Ottoman era – The Bursa example," *Uludağ University Faculty of Theology Journal*. Bursa, 2006, v:15, number 2, p. 304.
[127] Montagu, pp. 93-97.
[128] Grealde, p. 90.

er for aristocratic women and those form the lower classes to do so.[129] Society marginalized women who were divorced or abandoned by their husbands. There was a definite stigma associated with divorced women that there was not for men.[130]

As Kathryn Gleadle argues in her book *British Women in Nineteenth Century*, divorce for British women in the 19th century was tantamount to social exclusion and even separation from their children.[131]

The divorce process in the 19th century, and in prior centuries, was completely different in the Ottoman Empire and Britain. As per Catholic teachings, divorce was seen as a sin for many centuries in Christian societies. Starting from the eighth century, most Western societies saw marriage as sacrosanct, with the Catholic Church banning divorce even if couples had irreconcilable differences, or there were other sound reasons that prevented the couple from living together. A natural consequence of this ban was the rule that everyone would marry once in his or her lifetime. Marriage was seen as a sacrament given before God, with any attempt to annul such an agreement seen as a most grievous sin. In 1563, with the Council of Trent, divorce was accepted as an unalterable sin for believers.[132]

This decision was one of the factors that allowed the Protestant Reformation to spread throughout Europe. In the 16th century, King Henry VIII of England wanted to divorce his wife Catherine of Aragon, who had failed to produce him male heir, and marry Anne Boleyn. At the time, divorce was impossible even for the king of England. The resulting crisis ended only when Henry VIII severed ties with the Catho-

---

[129] ibid., p. 90.
[130] Yalom, p. 188.
[131] Grealde, p. 85.
[132] Yalom, p. 46.

lic Church and founded the Church of England in 1531, with himself as its head. Still, the right to divorce, granted to the king, was not allowed to the rest of the country. The king had no intention to grant ordinary people the right to divorce.[133]

In the following centuries, divorce in England was allowed only when a special dispensation was granted by the church and under the sole condition that the wife was unfaithful to her husband. Women, however, could not seek divorce for the same reason.

The application needed approval from British Parliament to be legitimate and the finalization of the divorce. The prohibitive cost of such a process precluded its use by anyone but the richest aristocrats.[134] This continued until 1857, when the Matrimonial Causes Act allowed women to file for divorce from their husbands. However, while men could cite only a case of infidelity for divorce, women had to prove infidelity, abuse, rape, or even incest before securing a legal separation.[135] While women were granted the right to divorce in 1857, they still faced many practical obstacles. The only court that saw divorce cases was in London, preventing its widespread use by those in rural areas with limited means.[136] Even as late as 1923, women had the right to file for divorce only if their husbands were unfaithful.[137] Until 1926, the only divorce court in Britain was located in London.[138]

In 19th century Britain, especially in the first half, marriage was seen as an indissoluble union that could only be broken with the death of a spouse. The reform movement

---

[133] ibid., p. 108.
[134] ibid., p. 120.
[135] Perkin, *Victorian Women*, p. 126.
[136] ibid., p.126.
[137] ibid., p. 126.
[138] ibid., p. 126.

against the Catholic Church produced a method that allowed church courts to grant couples a legal separation, but not divorce.[139] In Britain, as well as in Italy, France, and Germany, legal separation could be granted in cases of a woman's unfaithfulness or a man's physical abuse of his wife. The Russian Orthodox Church refused to grant a document of legal separation even in cases of physical abuse of a wife.[140]

However, as legal separation did not mean divorce, the separated man and woman could not legally marry someone else.[141] The only means for those who wanted to get remarried was to apply to Parliament, which was the only body that could object to the church's decision. Such a process cost an excessive amount of time and money, which was discouraging to most. The average process cost between 800 and 900 pounds sterling, money enough for the upkeep of a middle-class family for three years.[142]

It is no wonder that only 3 percent of all women in Britain applied to Parliament for divorce in the first half of the 19th century.[143] Wealthy aristocracy preferred to go through Parliament while members of the middle and lower classes were largely kept out of this process due to the cost.

The lower classes, which often had more flexible relations to religion and it moral dictates, found their own solution to the problem, which the more religious middle class frowned upon. Working-class couples that wanted to separate often did so without feeling the necessity to apply for a legal separation, employing symbolic acts instead. The cou-

---

[139] Perkin, *Women and Marriage in Nineteenth Century England*. p. 22.
[140] Rachel G. Fuchs, and Victoria E. Thompson, p. 56.
[141] Perkin, *Women and Marriage in Nineteenth Century England*. p. 22.
[142] Yalom, p. 186.
[143] ibid., p. 186.

ple would jump backward over a broom or just remove their rings.[144]

Another technique was "wife selling," a practice dating back to 1073. While extremely rare, for wife selling, a husband who wanted a divorce would place an ad in the local broadsheet announcing his intention to sell his wife. The person who bid the most would get the wife while the man would in essence be divorced. Gleadle explains it would take the mutual consent of both the husband and wife for wife selling to proceed.[145]

Perkin points out that the church ignored the practice of wife selling.[146] For instance, in 1814, working-class man Henry Cook was forced to marry a woman he was involved with in accordance with the Bastardy Law. Soon afterward, he placed his wife and child in an asylum. The local church official who ran the asylum had no intention of paying for their maintenance and asked Cook to sell his wife. The local church records show that Cook's wife was sold at auction for one shilling and that the church donated a lamb's leg to cover the cost of the sale and the wedding.[147]

The members of the middle class often criticized such demeaning actions. Thomas Hardy's 1886 novel *The Mayor of Casterbridge* begins with such an act. By the end of the 19th century, the lower classes joined in the criticism thanks to the activism of the women's rights movement, with men trying to sell their wives finding themselves attacked by the public with stones, mud, garbage, and even a dead dog.[148]

Divorce was far from frequent in the first half of the 19th

---

[144] Gleadle, p. 44.
[145] ibid., p. 44-45; Perkin, *Victorian Women*. p. 127.
[146] Gleadle, p. 44-45.
[147] Perkin, Victorian Women, p. 127.
[148] Perkin, Victorian Women, p. 128.

century, and when practiced, was almost exclusively limited to wealthy aristocrats.[149] This continued in Britain until 1857, with France legalizing divorce in 1884, and Germany having legalized divorce 100 years earlier in 1784. Italian women had to wait until the 20th century for the right to divorce their husbands.[150]

Divorce remained taboo, preventing officials from taking action that would protect the rights of women upon separation. Marital discord usually resulted in the husband leaving and the woman facing financial dire straits. Especially among the British lower classes, the occurrence of men leaving their wives and children behind was common. Women and children were often left destitute. Officials would try to find the husband and force him through the court to pay for the living expenses of his wife and children, but usually, they could not be found. Men would flee to a different country or live under an assumed name in a different region of Britain. Sometimes couples, again especially among the lower classes, would agree to privately separate and live with others.[151]

Failed marriages among the more religious middle classes would usually result in the couple living separately without a legal divorce, and many would try to get a document of legal separation. A woman whose husbands had left could not remarry because they still were legally married, unless they could prove their husband was dead.[152]

Women with marital troubles could not stay at their relatives if the husband legally objected. A woman who did not want to live with her husband could be legally forced to stay, practically as a prisoner in her own home. According to an

---

[149] Yalom, p. 188.
[150] Rachel G. Fuchs, and Victoria E. Thompson, p. 56.
[151] Perkin, *Victorian Women*, p. 127; Perkin, *Women and Marriage in Nineteenth Century England*. p. 115.
[152] Perkin, *Women and Marriage in Nineteenth Century England*, p. 22.

example from 1836, Cecilia Maria Cochrane decided to leave her husband after three years of marriage, taking her children and moving into her mother's house. Her husband, under the guise of a meeting to discuss legal separation, invited her home and refused to let her go. The woman filed a complaint at court, which decided that her husband, without resorting to violence, had the right to imprison her in the house.[153] The husband's right to forcefully imprison his wife was rescinded only with an act of Parliament in 1884.[154]

British women could not file for divorce based on irreconcilable differences until 1969. Despite successive legal improvements, lack of practical progress explains why the feminist movement never weakened throughout this era. Mona Caird's article published in the Westminster Review journal in 1888 on what women suffer attracted great interest, and it received 27,000 letters in response within two months. These letters provide a good summary of what British women had to go through to get a divorce. One letter from a woman demands the expansion of divorce rights:

> I must say I concur in the suggestion that greater facilities should be afforded for divorce. Let me cite my own case. My husband is a helpless drunkard. It is true, he earns a good living and keeps me in comparative luxury; but is this an adequate consideration for the fact that I have to associate with a drunken, besotted husband five nights out of seven? LUCRETIA, Westbourne Park, Aug. 20.[155]

Another was from a woman who is physically abused who cannot legally get a divorce:

> I am one of those who have most unhappily found marriage a

---

[153] Perkin, *Victorian Women*, p. 119.
[154] ibid.; Yalom, pp. 185-186.
[155] Yalom, p. 270.

most dismal failure. Married when only a girl, after a few years I am practically a widow, having been obliged, from my husband's brutality, to seek a separation. This was not until, through his brutality, I lost an eye, principally owing to the very merciful law which compelled me to live with a man until I was maimed for life. . . . M.S., Bedford Street, Strand, Aug. 21. [156]

One criticizes the failure of British laws to grant women the right to control their own properties:

> Another case of "Failure" in marriage is the objection English husbands have to their wives being independent in money matters. . . . Few men realise how humiliating it is to a woman of independent spirit to ask for every sixpence, nor the spirit of bitterness and rebellion that it engenders. . . . A LOST LIFE, Darenth, Kent, Sept. 26.[157]

Women in Western societies were also victimized when it came to alimony and the custody of children. Once married, the ownership of a woman's property passed on to her husband. However, after a divorce, unless she had a father or brother who would look after her, women became destitute. Women from the lower classes depended on social aid. What is worse, women had no right to ask back for what they brought to the marriage, money or property. However, the husband had the right to leave her penniless on the streets.[158]

Famous 19th century writers such as Jane Austen and Charlotte Bronte based their novels on such social inequalities.

It took the 1857 Divorce Act for British women to enjoy rights akin to those enjoyed by Muslim women in Islamic lands, for instance the right to demand funds such as *mihr*

---

[156] Yalom, p. 271.
[157] ibid., p. 272.
[158] Perkin, *Victorian Women*.

to survive. Until the 1878 Matrimonial Causes Act, divorced British women could not ask for alimony for themselves or their children.[159] Only in 1886 did courts decide that husbands had the obligation to provide for the wives they divorced or abandon and their children, with an upper limit of two pounds a week.[160]

In the early 19th century, children were seen as the wards of their father and, upon divorce, a mother had no right to ask for their custody or even see them. However, the Infants and Child Custody Act that British Parliament passed in 1839, thanks to the efforts of feminist activists, finally granted women the right to seek custody of their children under the age of seven and demand visitation rights for children under the age of 16. [161]

Before this law, the only way a divorced woman could get the custody of her children was if the husband was dead. In certain cases, husbands could even deny their ex-wives access to their children, which was a tragedy for both women and small children.

What forced public attention to this injustice and allowed the passage of the bill was what happened to Caroline Norton. At the age of 19 she married George Norton, an aristocrat. Her diaries are full of entries detailing the physical abuse she suffered at the hands of her husband. During the nine years of marriage, she often fled to her mother's home. Knowing that her husband would get custody of their children if she divorced, she returned back to her husband every time. Her husband, who was constantly low on funds himself,

---

[159] ibid., p. 122.
[160] Perkin, *Women and Marriage in Nineteenth Century England*, p. 116; Perkin, *Victorian Women*. pp. 130-139.
[161] Yalom, p. 186.

would take all the money she earned from writing for women's magazines that paid for for household needs. The couple finally separated, with the husband refusing to allow her to see their three children. Moreover, because the money she earned was legally her husband's, she was refused access to it. Caroline Norton, whose father was a playwright, in 1837, finally wrote the article "The Natural Claim of a Mother in the Custody of her Child as affected by the Common Law Right of the Father", which drew the attention of a member of Parliament. Still, the House of Lords rejected a proposed bill. Later, she used a male sobriquet to write a new bill, which passed as the 1839 Infant Custody Act. This law allowed divorced women, who were not unfaithful to their husbands, access to children under the age of one and the right to seek the custody of children under the age of seven.[162]

On the other hand, Edward Lane's observations in Cairo demonstrated that courts governed by Hanafi rules in Islamic countries automatically granted the custody of boys under the age of seven and girls under the age of nine to the mother, and fathers were obligated to pay for the costs of the children through alimony.[163]

In his 1836 book, Lane says:

A divorced woman who has a son under two years of age may retain him until he has attained that age, and may be compelled to do so by the law of the Shafe'ees; and, by the law of the Malikees, until he has arrived at puberty; but the yanafee law limits the period during which the boy should remain under her care to seven years : her daughter she should retain until nine years of age, or the period of puberty. If a man divorce his wife before

---

[162] Perkin, *Victorian Women*. p. 116.
[163] Seyd, pp. 79-81.

the consummation of marriage, he must pay her half the sum which he has promised to give her as a dowry ; or, if he have promised no dowry, he must pay her the half of the smallest dowry allowed by law, which has been above mentioned; and she may marry again immediately.[164]

Lane's observations are confirmed by court registries from Cairo at around the same time, with the custody of children given to mothers and fathers ordered to pay alimony for their children.[165]

For example, a Hanafi *qadi* decided to give a woman named Amna, daughter of Ibrahim, the custody of her son Abu Zeyd until the boy came of age. The father was ordered to pay the Amna half a *fidda*.[166]

Harvey, who was in Constantinople in 1878, argues that marriage in Islam is not a sanctified act before God as it is in Christianity, but a social contract.

Marriage in Turkey is not a religious ceremony; it is merely a civil covenant that can be annulled for very trivial reasons by either party. Public opinion, however, pronounces such separations disgraceful, and they are seldom resorted to unless for grave reasons. A man can put away his wife by pronouncing before a third person that his marriage is "void," but must in that case resign all the property that his wife has ever possessed. A woman can only obtain a divorce by going before a cadi, and declaring that she yields all her dower and property, and claims her freedom. Should there be children, the mother, if she so elects, can retain the girls with her until they are seven years old; after that age they return to their father's house, unless an especial arrangement has been made to the contrary. [167]

---

[164] Lane, p. 101.
[165] Abdal-Rehim, pp. 108-109.
[166] ibid.
[167] Harvey, pp. 70-71.

CONCLUSION

While many of the travel books Western authors in the 19th century wrote about the East can be included among works Edward Said criticizes for being prejudicial in the context of the theory of orientalism. One must admitted, however, that there were also some who tried to remain objective and understand the other. Women formed the majority of travelogue writers with more tolerant attitudes, providing an alternative to the male dominant orientalist books based on imperialist ideologies.

Still, as this book demonstrates, there were also male travelogue writers who visited the Ottoman Empire and wrote their unprejudiced and sound observations of Eastern societies. And it would be wrong to dismiss out of hand travelogues written by men, anyway. It must be kept in mind that any assessment of these travelogues should analyze how gender differences affect perception of the other, and that sometimes, one's experiences and political and religious beliefs, without any gender-based baggage, can become an important factor in the definition of the other.

This study does not constitute a stance against Said's findings. In fact, it is just the opposite. The purpose of this study is to place the issue on sounder footing by examining how orientalist rhetoric changes color and multiplies depending on the way Western travel writers perceive Ottoman women and society.

In this context, I aimed to compile trends that provide an alternative to the orientalist outlook when it comes to women's status in Ottoman society, marriage, life in the harem, and divorce with references from different travelogues.

Additionally, in light of the observations by19th century Western travelers provide, I aimed to underline certain issues, through which the East looks at itself through an orientalist lens. The compilation of such information from Western sources is also important to those of us who want to challenge the Western narrative that created orientalism. That's why the section on the status of Ottoman women through observations by Westerners was included, as were the marital, divorce, and custodial rights enjoyed by British women of the time.

With the information gathered from travelogues, this study allows us to reach certain conclusions on the life and status of women in Ottoman society.

Contrary to general opinion, women were not imprisoned in harems in the Ottoman Empire. As many Western travelers saw firsthand, Ottoman women were free to go about in the streets. Ottoman women could go to hamams, travel to local excursion spots, and visit friends. Also, married and divorced Ottoman women enjoyed much greater financial and legal security compared to British women of the time. Unlike their British counterparts, Ottoman women had the right to file for divorce and did not face legal discrimination and social exclusion once divorced.

I can confidently assert as a result of this study that Western women only began in late 19th century to enjoy marital and divorce rights similar to their counterparts in the East under Islamic law. While the exact opposite seems to be true in much of the Middle East now, it would be wrong to judge the millennia-long history of the region by the 21st century socio-cultural states of affairs, which are the product of Western powers' colonialist policies of the past few centuries.

The lack of knowledge about the rights Islam grants to women or the narrow-minded reflexes of male-dominant societies are to blame for the present marital or divorce difficulties faced by women in the region.

In addition to many indirect causes of the deterioration of the status of women in the Middle East, the main reason behind it is the breakdown in Islamic societies and the failure to properly learn the basic tenets of Islam, as 19th century Islamic reformer, Egyptian jurist Mohammed Abdu, plainly identified at the time.

As this book argues, the rights and privileges granted by the Ottoman Empire, one of the greatest Islamic states in history, were second to none until very recently, and hopefully contributes to put many prejudicial assumptions to rest.

REFERENCES

Abdal-Rehim, Abdal-Rehim Abdal-Rahman. "The Family and Gender Laws in Egypt During the Ottoman Period," Amira El Azhary Sonbol (ed.), *Women, the Family, and Divorce Laws in Islamic History*, Syracuse: Syracuse University Press, 1996, pp. 96-111.

Ahmed, Leila. "Early, Islam and the Position of Women: The Problem of Interpretation," *Women in Middle Eastern History*, New York: Vail-Ballou Press, 1991, pp. 58-74.

Al-Khalaf, Moodhy. "Islamic Tradition Proves that the Women Have the Right to Be Leaders," Margaet Speaker Yuan (ed.), *Women in Islam*, Detroit: Greenhaven Press, 2005, pp. 29-34.

Altick, Richard, D. *Victorian People and Ideas*, New York: W.W. Norton & Company Inc., 1973.

Ashcroft, Bill, and Pal Ahluwalia. *Edward Said (Routledge Critical Thinkers)* (2. ed.), New York: Routledge, 2009.

Aydın, M. Akif. *Islam and Ottoman Family Law*, Istanbul: Marmara University Publishing, 1988, pp. 69, 103-104.

Berkey, Jonathan P. "Women and Islamic Education in the Mamluk Period," *Women in Middle Eastern History*, New York: Vail-Ballou Press, 1991, pp. 143-161.

Blower, Sally. "The Smallpox Story: Life and Death of an Old Disease," Microbiology Review, 47 (4), 1983, pp. 455-509.

Calder, Jenni. *Women and Marriage in Victorian Fiction*, London: Thames and Hudson, 1976.

Davis, Fanny. *The Ottoman Lady: A Social History from 1718 to 1918*, New York: Greenwood Press, 1986.

Diamond, Jared. *1000 Events that Shaped the World*, Washington: National Geographic Society, 2007.

Fargues, Philippe. "Family and Household in Mid-Nineteenth Century Cairo," Beshara Doumani (ed.), *Family History in the Middle East: Hosuehold, Property, and Gender*, New York: State University of New York Press, 2003, pp. 23-51.

Edward, Said. *Orientalism*, New York: Vintage Books, 1994.

Fuchs, Rachel G., and Victoria E. Thompson. *Women in Nineteenth Century Europe*. New York: Palgrave Macmillan, 2005.

Gleadle, Kathryn. *British Women in the Nineteenth Century*. New York: Palgrave, 2001.

Hamid, Halil. *The Diary of a Turk*, London: Adam and Charles Black. 1903.

Harvey, Annie Jane. *Turkish Harems and Circassian Home*. London: Hurst and Blackett, 1871.

Hornby, Emilia Bithynia. *In and Around Stamboul*. Philadelphia: James Challen & Son, 1918 (1st ed. 1858).

Jalland, Pat. *Women, Marriage and Politics 1860-1914*. Oxford: Oxford University Press, 1986.

Jennings, Ronald C. "Women in Early 17th Century Ottoman Judicial Records: The Sharia Court of Anatolian Kayseri." *Journal of the Economic and Social History of the Orient*, Vol. 18, No. 1 (Jan. 1975), pp. 53-114.

Karaman, Hayrettin. *Mukayeseli İslâm Hukuku I-II-III*. İstanbul: İz Yayıncılık, 2009.

King, Donald, and Sylvester David, eds. *The Eastern Carpet in the Western World, From the 15th to the 17th century*. London: Arts Council of Great Britain, 1983.

Kuno, Kenneth. "Disobedient Wives and Neglectful Husbands." *Family, Gender, and Law in a Globalizing Middle East and South Asia*. Syracuse: Syracuse University Press, 2009, p. 3-19.

Montagu, Mary Wortley. *Letters of Lady Mary Wortley Montagu*. Sarah Josepha Hale, ed. Boston: Roberts Brothers, 1869.

Lane, Edward William. *The Manners and Customs of the Modern Egyptians* (23rd ed.), London: J. M. Dent and Co., 1908 (1st ed. 1836).

Levine, Philippa. *Victorian Feminism 1850-1900*. Tallahassee: The Florida State University Press, 1987.

Lewis, Reina. *Gendering Orientalism; Race, Femininity and Representation*. London: Routledge, 1996.

Malouf, Greg and Lucy. *A Chef's Travels in Turkey*. California: Chronicle Books, 2008.

Maydaer, Saadet. "Osmanlı Klasik Döneminde Kadınların Servet Edinme Yolları (Bursa Örneği)." *Uludağ Üniversitesi İlahiyat Fakültesi Dergisi*. Bursa, cilt: 15, sayı: 2, 2006, pp. 365-381.

Maydaer, Saadet. "Klasik Dönem Osmanlı Toplumunda Boşanma (Bursa Şeriyye Sicillerine Göre)." *Uludağ Üniversitesi İlahiyat Fakültesi Dergisi*. Bursa, v: 16, n: 1, 2007, pp. 299-320.

Melman, Billie. *Women's Orients: English Women and the Middle East, 1718-1918*. Ann Arbor: The University of Michigan Press, 1992.

Mills, Sarah. *Discourses of Difference: An Analysis of Women's Travel Writing and Colonialism.* London: Routledge, 1993.

Monroe, Will Seymour. *Turkey and the Turks.* Boston: Colonial Press, 1907.

Murray, John. *Handbook for Travellers in Constantinople and Turkey in Asia.* (4. ed.), London: John Murray Firm, 1878.

Napier, E. Colonel. *Excursions Along the Shores of the Mediterranean, vol. II.* London: Henry Colburn Publisher, 1842.

Nashat, Guity, and Judith Tucker. *Women in the Middle East and North Africa.* Bloomington: Indiana University Press, 1998.

Pane, Michael. *The Crusades: History and Myths Revealed.* New York: Fall River Press, 2009.

Pardoe, Julia. *The City of the Sultan and Domestic Manners of the Turks with a Steam Voyage up to Danube.* (4. ed.), London: G. Routledge & Co., 1854.

Perkin, Joan. *Women and Marriage in Nineteenth Century England.* Chicago: Lyceum Books, 1989.

—. *Victorian Women.* New York: New York University Press, 1993.

Poole, Sophia. *The Englishwoman in Egypt: Letters From Cairo.* Azza Kararah (ed.), Egypt: The American University in Cairo Press, 2003.

—. *Culture and Imperialism.* London: Chatto & Windus, 1993.

—. *The World, The Text and The Criti.* Cambridge, MA: Harvard University Press, 1983.

Sancar, Aslı. *Ottoman Women: Myth and Reality.* New Jersey: The Light Inc., 2007.

Shanley, Mary Lyndon. *Feminism, Marriage and the Law in Victorian England.* New Jersey: Princeton University Press, 1989.

Slade, Admiral Adophous. *Records of Travels in Turkey and Greece and of a Cruise in the Black Sea with Captain Pasha.* 1833.

Smyth, Warrington W. *A Year with the Turks or Sketches of Travel in the European and Asiatic Dominions of the Sultan.* New York: Redfield, 1854.

Syed, Mohammad Ali. *The Position of Women in Islam: A Progressive View.* Albany: State University of New York Press, 2004.

Thackeray, William Makepeace. *Notes of a Journey from Cornhill to Grand Cairo.* New York: Wiley & Putnam, 1846.

Thornton, Lynne. *Women as Portrayed in Orientalist Painting.* Paris: ACR PocheCouleur, 1994.

Thurnber, Francis B. C. *Coffee from Plantation to Cup: A Brief History of Coffee Production and Consumption.* (9. ed.), New York: American Grocer Publishing Association, 1884.

Tucker, Judith. "Ties That Bound: Women and Family in Eighteenth and Nineteenth Century Nablus." *Women in Middle Eastern Histor.* New York: Vail-Ballou Press, 1991, pp. 233-254.

Yalom, Marilyn. *A History of the Wife.* New York: Harper Collins Publishers, 2001.

Wadud, Amina. "The Koran Teaches That Women Have the Same Rights as Men." Margaet Speaker Yuan (ed.), *Women in Islam.* Detroit: Greenhaven Press, 2005, pp. 9-14.

White, Charles. *Three Years in Constantinople or the Domestic Manners of the Turks in 1844, vol. II.* London: Henry Colburn, 1845.

Zarinebaf-Shahr, Fariba. "Women, Law, and Imperial Justice in Ottoman Istanbul in the Late Seventeenth Century." Amira El Azhary Sonbol (ed.), *Women, the Family, and Divorce Laws in Islamic History.* Syracuse: Syracuse University Press, 1996, pp. 81-95.